BURY ME
with my fly rod

THE UNVARNISHED
TRUTH ABOUT FLY FISHING

Dennis D. Dauble
Illustrations by Ronald Reed

FishHead Press
Richland, WA

Illustrations by Ronald Reed
Book Design by Keokee

Published by:
FishHead Press
3029 Sonoran Drive
Richland, WA 99354
www.DennisDaubleBooks.com

In cooperation with:
Keokee Co. Publishing, Inc.
405 Church Street
Sandpoint, ID 83864
(208) 263-3573
www.keokeebooks.com

Cover and interior photos by author.

ISBN: 9781096465966

FLY FISHING IS GORY AMUSEMENT
-RUDYARD KIPLING

DO NOT TELL FISH STORIES WHERE THE PEOPLE KNOW YOU;
BUT PARTICULARLY, DON'T TELL THEM WHERE
THEY KNOW THE FISH.
-MARK TWAIN

CONTENTS

A fly rod and overstuffed box of flies take a break alongside
the Deschutes River.

Introduction

IN LATE SUMMER 2009, I opened the front door of our home to find a long, skinny cardboard box leaning up against the porch wall. The return address on the box read: "Trout Unlimited Headquarters." Inside was a stainless steel rod case embossed with "R.L. Winston Rod Company. Fine Rods Since 1929. Twin Bridges, Montana." Unscrewing the elegant brass top, I slid out a soft cotton liner that protected a four-piece rod with serial numbers etched in cursive above each ferrule. The rod blank was mallard drake green and glowed iridescent in the afternoon light. I recall a feeling like winning the lottery.

Sleep came in fits and starts that night as I reflected on the long road traveled since my first fly fishing outfit, a 6-foot Berkley spinning rod and open-face spinning reel that served me well for my formative years. Backing, fly line, and tippet consisted of drugstore monofilament. No. 20 Light Cahills and No. 18 Adams did not populate my box of hand-me-down flies. I favored large attractor-type patterns, typically tied with deer hair, because they helped me cast farther.

A six-piece spin/fly combo rod increased my angling arsenal when I backpacked the Wallowa Mountains as a Boy Scout. The rod responded slowly during hook sets but had sufficient backbone to tire a 10-inch brook trout. Six basic patterns filled my box of flies until well after high school: Gray Hackle, Brown Hackle, Renegade, Bucktail Royal Coachman, Wilson, and Caddis. They were easy to tie and caught fish whether fished wet or dry. Such terms as emergers, spinners and duns didn't enter my vocabulary until much later.

When my older brother, Dusty, inherited Grandpa Harry's prized bamboo fly rod, he passed his trusty Shakespeare Wonder Rod down the line to me. Thrilled with the upgrade in equipment, I was too naïve to know I got the short end of the deal. Fly rod number three was a 4-weight fiberglass Fenwick I built to battle redside rainbows on Oregon's Crooked River. By then, I was married, Nancy was pregnant with our first child and frugality was the first order of business.

It's not like Nancy and I cut up a hotdog five ways to get through the week, but inexpensive fly rods and budget reels stayed the norm until she shed her stay-at-home role and returned to the work force. Blame my frugality on a childhood upbringing that taught me to take what you get and make the best of it. The first indication of my pocketbook loosening up led to a 7-weight Cortland rod and matching large arbor reel for targeting steelhead on the Hanford Reach of the Columbia River. The floodgates opened when I purchased a 9-foot, 6-weight trout rod on inventory clearance and a four-piece 5-weight using a gift certificate. A more recent indulgence – blame it on peer pressure – led to the purchase of a slightly used two-hand Spey rod.

Given this economical background, how did a state-of-the-art, 5-weight boron fly rod end up on my rod rack? Why would someone having a long history of bargain fly rods aspire to such a fine piece of equipment? The bold move can be traced back to a friend, when offered a large cash bonus to retire early, took the money, bought a new pickup truck, and never looked back. I held onto the idea of my company offering up a similar sweetheart deal, but they weren't handing out severance packages when I checked out from the work place. What I did have up my sleeve, however, was a stockpile of vacation hours, enough to give myself a five-figure "bonus." Sometimes you have to look out for number one.

I thought long and hard about what to do with the windfall. Ideally, it would be spent on something that my heirs would fight over during the reading of the will. In the midst of my careful deliberation, a promotional letter arrived from Trout Unlimited. *Get in line behind the last twenty charities and conservation groups who hit me up six times a year*, I thought, when I opened the letter. The clincher in the pitch for a lifetime membership, was a Winston rod and matching Lamson reel. To make a long story short, I wrote off the contribution and ended up with a rod and reel I had only imagined. *Ain't retirement grand?*

Alas, any new rod in your fly-fishing arsenal begs important questions, starting with when and where do you take the first cast? And these questions ramp up relative to its cost. For example, do you protect the rod like a rare sports car with a custom paint job? Do you bring it out only for special occasions, like fine China? Or do you use it as an everyday rod while your aging legs are still strong enough to hike backcountry trails and wade swift mountain streams?

One thing is for sure. At the rate I acquire top-tier fishing equipment, the Winston rod and companion reel are destined to be family heirlooms. This admission leads to the challenge of whom to pass the outfit to. My first thought is to skip a generation and bequeath the rod and reel to a special grandchild – an idea not shared with either my son or daughter. Both would break the other's right arm to get it. Should the Winston go to the oldest grandchild, Liam; a game boy whiz at age 10, who programmed my cell phone to ring a Taj Mahal tune with the lyrics "going fishing?" Or, should it go to Annalise, the first of four grandchildren to land a feisty rainbow trout on a fly rod? Admittedly, I hooked the fish, but she was only 4 years old and reeled it in all by herself. Or should the rod and reel go to fearless Sofia? She's as independent as her mother and never wants to be left behind when it comes to fishing. Then there's the youngest grandson, Adam. This "fishing boy" casts a 3-weight with either hand and can sense the presence of rising trout from 100 feet away.

This digression is merely thinking ahead, because between now and when I reach the last fishing hole in the sky, I plan to catch as many native rainbow trout as possible with my Winston fly rod. Farther down the road, I hope my grandchildren will taxi this "Papa D" to his home waters, just as I transported my Grandpa Harry to the South Fork of the Walla Walla River after the keys to his '65 Ranchero were taken away. I imagine warm summer afternoons hiking tree-lined trails, sharing cookies and chips, and telling fish stories.

Not to intimidate interested family members, but if these imaginations are not realized, they might as well bury me with my fly rod.

If I had only one fly pattern to cast for rainbow trout in my home water, it would be a Stimulator.

Part One. Blue Mountain Waters

On the south side of the columbia......
lies a ridge of blue hills, well wooded,
sending out many brooks and rivulets
and 2 or 3 bold rivers....

-David Thompson 8 July 1811

BURY ME with my fly rod

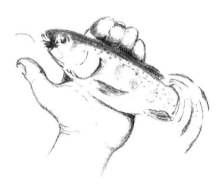

Where Speckled Trout Live

There's a steamy scene in the epic World War I movie "The Blue Max" where Ursula Andress perches on the edge of a bed wearing nothing but a tiny terrycloth towel. A teenager at the time, I remember praying for the towel to drop and reveal her ample charms, but it must have been glued on. Unfortunately, that movie scene flashed in my head when my 80 year-old mother-in-law, clad only in a worn bath towel, pushed her walker up to the front door of her home to let me in. With one hand clutching the corner of her towel and the other on the doorknob, the situation appeared as unstable as a Middle East peace pact.

"Uh, oh, Betty," I blurted, leaning back on my heels from the front door stoop. "I should have called to warn you that I was coming."

"That's okay. I was just getting out of the bath when the doorbell rang and didn't want to miss your visit," she replied.

"Tell you what. You go ahead and get dressed and I'll stop by on my way back from fishing."

"Okay. See you then."

Before I could close the door and turn away, Betty shuffled her walker around to expose a wrinkled backside.

Still trying to purge the daunting image of Betty's disobedient towel out of my mind, I push down the top strand of a barbed wire fence that impedes my approach to a small pasture that adjoins Couse Creek. Unfortunately, my wading shorts catch on a cruel barb. Withdrawal involves precarious posturing, one leg stuck out like a dog marking his territory, and the other on tiptoe, like a ballerina. My goal for the day had been to avoid compromising situations and without making a single cast I had already encountered two. Fishing should not be that difficult.

Couse Creek is what stream ecologists call a first-order stream. The southernmost tributary to the Walla Walla River, it originates at an elevation of 3,000-feet, where Lincton and Basket Mountain ridges calve off the western slope of the Blues. To put things in perspective, Couse Creek is three steps wide and no more than thigh-deep. Two people can't fish together in such tight quarters without disturbing its small population of trout. As a consequence, I rarely invite anyone along. Self-centered is often the most practical form of human behavior.

As a relentless teenager, I crawled under these same pasture fences, working stealthily through blackberry vines and stinging nettles in search of a 10-trout limit of "six-inchers." Although these early experiences paved the way for catching bigger trout in bigger water, the thrill of fooling small fish in small water has never waned. My current visit to Couse Creek focuses on getting a fix of black-speckled rainbow trout from its steel-blue water. It's not so much how many or how large the fish, but the opportunity to go back in time that attracts me.

At its confluence with the Walla Walla River, five miles upstream of the city of Milton-Freewater, Oregon, the opening to Couse Creek is less than 200 yards wide. The surrounding slopes are mostly bare of vegetation except for swatches of cheat grass and tumble mustard. The first thing you notice after turning off the river road is a metal-span bridge that affords access to a small park named after Marie Dorion. "Madam Dorion" was an Iowan Indian who traveled west with members of the Wilson Hunt party to the "Oualla-Oualla" River valley during the winter of 1811. Concrete steps, chiseled with the names of early pioneers, climb a steep hill overlooking a former mill site. I picked Italian plums and Bing cherries from nearby orchards with my buddy Norm and his Dad when I was in high school. We'd freeze a gallon jug full of drinking water, cash in our bucket of fruit at noon, and go fishing until we caught enough trout for dinner.

The narrow asphalt road leading up Couse Creek swoops like a roller-coaster ride. Stream flow is hidden behind a screen of alder and elderberry that shelters songbirds and the occasional racoon. Nested in a grove of black locust is a pair of singlewide trailers. Rusty car bodies and discarded farming equipment lay in confused angles across a gravel turnaround driveway. Welcome to rural eastern Oregon.

A mile farther down the road, a whitewashed farmhouse showcases neat rows of strawberries in a backyard garden. The crossroad here leads to lower Basket Mountain Road and the heart of the Blues for those willing to four-wheel it. "Road Closed

Dec 1st – March 1st. Primitive Road No Warning." I prowled these deep-rutted ridge roads in high school, sipping cheap beer, hoping to cop a feel, and watching for the county sheriff's headlights.

Century Farm, a secluded streamside property held dear by the same family since 1860, comes up next through your windshield. Farther upstream is my "secret" fishing spot – one of a handful of places that lack a "No Trespassing" sign. Pretty much everything else has been posted up tight for years. Which reminds me of the time I got kicked off private property a mile or so down the road.

The scene played out on a sunny day in late May, when admittedly, an empty creel came into play. Tossing normal caution aside, I crow-hopped over a barbed wire fence and bee-lined for uncharted water, figuring to harvest a brace of trout. Keeping a low profile, I stayed in the cover of streamside willow and fished my way downstream until a wood-frame farmhouse with a fresh coat of paint came into view.

Things got interesting when I headed back to my pickup. A battered Dodge truck backed out of the farmhouse driveway and sped across the newly plowed field fast enough to send dirt clods flying. The driver, a short stocky man wearing a sheepskin-lined denim jacket, jumped out of the truck and confronted me. A black cowboy hat pulled down tight did not hide his beet-red face. "What the hell are you doing on my property?" he yelled.

The landowner's neck muscles twitched like a power lifter. His posture reminded me of a high school bully who caught me talking to his girlfriend. I sensed he wanted to kick my ass. The sight of his holstered Colt 45 led to my self-preservation instinct kicking in. Concerned that the angry man would shoot first and ask questions later, I spread my arms in mock surrender and said, "I was only fishing." Following that weak explanation was a promise to head straight out and never fish on his property again.

Momentarily deterred by my reticent response, the modern-day cowboy stared me down. It was during this defining moment that I took opportunity to skedaddle. Several giant steps later, I was safe in my truck.

Bringing myself back to present, I straighten my wading shorts and look around for a hell-bent landowner. As luck would have it, the only visible life forms are four horses that look up from their grazing. One is solid white, one palomino, one sorrel and one gray with a speckled rump. I wonder which horse Nancy would choose if she had a paddock to keep it in. I once made the mistake of buying her a used riding saddle with nice tooling; imagining it would make up for her not having a horse to call her own. *Maybe she could display it alongside her childhood collection of porcelain ponies (some with missing legs)?* Always the practical one, Nancy didn't think much of the gift. "What am I supposed to do with an old saddle?" she said. "Take it to a riding stable and hope it fits one of their ponies?"

Lucky for me, the grandkids like to ride Nana's "hitching post" when they visit the family cabin.

Due east of the horse pasture, a short draw drops steeply from the foothills of the Blue Mountains. The upper portion is pinched into a cursive "V." Open range – what locals call scabland – is mostly bare, except for scattered stands of buckbrush and smooth sumac that fill hillside pockets. Senescent balsamroot dot sloped ground, leaving the impression of a scraggly beard. Bachelor's buttons display pink and blue blooms beside a W-shaped split-rail fence. To the west, cultivated peas cover fields flat enough to be plowed. Some are knee high with succulent white blossoms as big as my thumb. Powerful combines will roll across the green fields like a battalion of Army tanks inside of a month.

I try to suppress the roller-coaster sense of urgency that floods my senses whenever I go trout fishing. Call it what you want, but I am anxious. I take a deep breath and delight in the coo of a mourning dove. A gust of wind rolls up the familiar sweet, musky odor of blooming cottonwood. Field grasses stir then stop, as if someone shut a door. The black-soil bottomland signals home. I am reminded of what I like best about small water: there are few secrets, only surprises.

I assemble my four-piece fly rod – the one that resides full-time under the backseat of my truck – and select a Renegade from a small collection of flies tied over the winter. Renegades are a classic pattern for western trout water. They have all the essential elements: white saddle hackle for visibility; brown saddle hackle for added buoyancy, contrast, and impression of movement; a body of iridescent peacock herl to attract. Renegades can be floated dry, bounced along the bottom, or drifted somewhere in between. Ninety percent of all self-respecting rainbow trout go for one on the first pass. *Why start with anything else?*

My next challenge is navigating tangled blackberry and honeysuckle vines that block my route to the creek via an old cow trail. I tuck Grandpa Harry's vintage creel under my armpit and slide sideways through the undergrowth to avoid stinging nettle that reach for my bare legs like hungry anemones. Reaching the creek, I adjust my polarized sunglasses to scope out a shallow run. The water runs slate-green and cloudy, but is clear enough to expose a medium-sized trout finning lazily next to a basalt outcrop. I crouch on one knee and flip a cast just upstream of where it holds. As if scripted, the fish turns and takes the fly. A brief run to the head of the pool and two jumps later it veers toward me as I apply pressure. I lift my rod tip and swing the trout flopping out of the water and pin it against my armpit. Without further thought, I deposit it headfirst into the top opening of Grandpa's creel. The instinct to harvest is sometimes too strong to ignore.

I kneel to return a cast. My Renegade floats softly through the air and settles on the water's surface where current swirls to create a foam line. A trout rises from the shadows and strikes the fly to battle at the head of the pool. Similar to the first fish, its backside and caudal fin are deeply speckled. Nickel-sized parr marks, bisected by a pencil-thin red stripe, contrast with gleaming silver flanks. This one I carefully unhook. It regains its breath in the shallows next to my feet, jerks upright, and sprints for the opposite bank. Satiated from my early success, I head upstream. The keeper trout flaps dully against the inside willow weave of Grandpa's creel.

It's easy to be entertained within the shadowy confines of Couse Creek. Water striders race across the water to demonstrate the subtle power of surface tension. The undersides of rocks crust with stonefly larvae, tiny snails and nubbly sponge. Shallow tailouts display caddisflies in pebble-lined cases, lined up like trailers in an RV park. Great blue herons pose on one leg, attempting to lull minnows into fatal complicity. Every trip to Couse Creek is like making love on a lazy afternoon; where casual study leads to reward.

Cutting across a sharp bend, I spook two whitetail doe that are bedded down for a noontime nap. Flagged tails held high in alarm, they crash through a maze of shoulder-high water hemlock and mullein. My ankles are bleeding from encounters with blackberry vines, but I want to catch more fish so I point my rod tip ahead, and weave through a crop of teasel that towers over my head.

Farther upstream is an undercut bank with trout written all over it. Unfortunately, overhanging willow creates a challenge. I pretend to be inanimate and drop my offering through a salad bowl-size opening. A small dark form rises from the depths but refuses my fly. I drop several more "casts" through jumbled deadfall, but the trout stays put. *Time to move on.*

A deep riffle yields a plump 8-incher. When the trout struggles to swim against the bend in my rod, another joins the chase. Seeing as how both fish came out of nowhere, I am reminded "just because you don't see 'em doesn't mean they ain't there." Figuring there are more than enough fish to support my modest intentions, I creel a second trout.

Every shift of the creek presents a scene as interesting as a small town bar on Saturday night. I find an old tractor tire wedged between elbow-shaped alder roots. Grapefruit-sized balls of foam collect in the far corner of a deep swirl pool and break loose when they reach the current edge. Sunlight spotlights a swarm of mayflies dancing above the water's surface. Honeysuckle vines sway over a shallow riffle like dreadlocks blowing in the wind. Lichens in subtle shades of green and brown cover a shaded rock outcrop.

Other features of the stream trigger fond memories. The corner pool, where my son, Matthew, caught his first stream trout at age six, has partially filled in, but the outline is still visible. I'll never forget his determined stance, narrow gaze, and his sense of purpose when he dangled a worm in that swirling back eddy; refusing to budge until he hooked the small bait-stealing trout.

Bringing trout to a fly isn't a problem for me today, although some places involve more creativity than others. As an example, one deep riffle affords no casting room because of overhanging alder. To place an offering where I imagine a trout lurks requires circling upstream and casting from the opposite shore. When nothing shows on the first pass, I mend my line to let the fly to drift under an overhang of reed canary grass. *Wham!* A 5-incher comes out of nowhere and clobbers my fly on the skid. Startled by the sudden assault, I send the trout flying over my shoulder onto the creek margin where it rests, gill plates flaring, until a gentle nudge with my toe snaps it out of its coma and it swims back to where it came from.

On one early season trip to Couse Creek, I kept track of my catch, stopping every 15 minutes or so to record the facts in a pocket journal. That day, 2 hours and 10 minutes of fishing produced 28 trout, ranging from 4- to 9-inches in length. My notes also documented that I lost the granddaddy of Couse Creek, a foot-long dark-speckled trout that resided under an exposed root wad. In a moment of inattention, I missed the hookset, pulling the fish to the surface for a "volitional release." Being slow on the draw is not limited to geriatric gunslingers.

The roof of an 80-year old farmhouse comes into view through a break in the streamside canopy to signal my visit is almost over. A wire fence that marks the property boundary functions more as a debris collector than a deterrent to trespassing though. Captured by loose strands of barbed wire are a microcosm of rural life: split firewood, rusty hot water tank, beer cans, ragged sweatshirt, garden hose, empty Purina dogfood sack, and, overtopping it all, like a maraschino cherry, a red plastic antifreeze container. Only in the hinterlands of the West does one farmer's junk create another man's fishing hole.

Downstream of the debris jam, a deep pool swirls languidly in the shade of a massive cottonwood tree. The cottonwood's ribbed trunk tilts precariously from a steep clay bank to expose massive roots. I embrace the tree like I would a weight challenged friend to pass. Standing atop the debris pile, I tie on a Golden Stimulator and cast to the downstream portion of the great hole. No sooner does my offering hit the water than a large trout – easily 14 inches long – rises and tries to "knock it out." I miss the broadside strike and, in my haste to return another cast, get hung up in overhanging alder. Luckily, I pull the fly free. Working the current edge slowly now, I let the fly sink and wait for a gentle pull or tap that signals a take.

Eventually, I give up and cast into a loose jumble of dead branches on the opposite shore. It is the kind of do-or-die cast made when your day is coming to an end and you need an excuse to quit. But, no sooner does the fluffed-up tuft of deer hair hit the surface than a big trout rolls on top of it. This time I set the hook and the fish churns downstream, fighting like a prizefighter on uppers. He is the Mike Tyson of Couse Creek. I hang on while he looks to serve a knockout punch. The battle includes head-shaking splashes, spinning twists, and one half-ass jump. Tight quarters are as much of a challenge for him as me – proving it's difficult to show off when you are confined by a straitjacket.

I work the big trout back to the middle of the hole, where he circles wildly. I reclaim slack line when he swims upstream, but he outsmarts me by burrowing into the debris pile beneath my feet. I move my rod tip gingerly to ease him out. I pull back with a sense of urgency. He refuses to budge. *No matter,* I think. *Keep your cool. Let out slack line (a technique I read about in a fishing article). Wait for him to swim out from his protective lair.* Those tactics prove ineffective, so I lie on my belly and pull on the leader by hand. That's when the loose pile of debris collapses and I find myself on my back in a foot of water.

The only witness to my foible is a red-tailed hawk riding a thermal in slow circles overhead. A quick inventory of body parts reveals no cuts, no broken bones. The only thing hurt is my feelings. Regardless, I find consolation in the knowing that Couse Creek still holds an occasional lunker trout. Well-timed rationalization is like a shot of adrenaline to a realist.

A narrow opening in blackberry vines leads me back to the horse pasture. Arriving at my truck, I savor the midday quiet. The scene is like a picture painted on canvas. Heat waves shimmer off hillside bedrock. A single cumulus cloud appears tethered to the horizon. Sapphire blue sky is stage backdrop to emerald green pea fields. Not a creature stirs, except for a lone raven that sidesteps nervously on the crosspiece of a nearby telephone pole. The words of Pulitzer Prize-winning author H.L. Davis came to mind: "There really is a sort of sustaining feeling about having a creek somewhere that other people don't know about, or in knowing something about it that they have missed."

Thankful to have been raised to *not* feel guilty about harvesting an occasional trout, I transfer my catch to small lunch cooler. One for me and one for Betty (who should be dressed by now). My mood is best described as melancholy. But, mostly, I feel a gratefulness that comes with the good fortune that has allowed me to visit that same tiny creek over a span of four decades, a place where every trip leads to discovery.

BURY ME with my fly rod

Spirit Mountain

THE SEED FOR MY FIRST hike-and-fish adventure to the Wenaha River found fertile ground after I planted the idea on two long-time friends during a microbrew moment. Of all trout streams whose headwaters originate in the Blue Mountains, the Wenaha River had eluded me despite rumors of rainbow trout and bull trout as long as your arm.

Maybe I lived in the past, but a 16-mile backpacking trip didn't seem like that big of a deal. My credentials include a Boy Scout merit badge that required hiking 50 miles of backcountry trail. I can cook a three-course meal over wood coals and don't mind sleeping on the ground. My vintage pack frame hung in the garage, itching to hit the trail. Admittedly, it had been more than a dozen years since I tested my ability, that on a backpacking trip into the Eagle Cap Wilderness of the Wallowa Mountains with my son Matthew.

My two fishing buddies and I prepared for the early August trip to the Wenaha River in different ways. Ted got in shape hiking up and down Badger Mountain with a pack full of rocks. I carried my clubs around the golf course for several rounds. Ken, a regular visitor to a court club, followed his wife around the shopping mall prior to our departure. Otherwise, we relied on zip-off leg pants for everyday wear, closed-toe sandals for wading, and trusted that our ancient Boy Scout mess kits still had utility.

The Wenaha-Tucannon Wilderness Area is rugged country, with over 200 miles of managed trails and several tributary streams to explore. The larger landscape was shaped, in part by lava flows that inundated the region around 16 million years ago. According to geologists, subsequent uplifting of the Blue Mountains into a broad arch caused the rivers to down-cut the steep, deep canyons that are evident today. The Wenaha River skirts the southern edge of the Wilderness Area, flowing eastward from the Blues and dropping in elevation nearly 4,000 feet from its origin near Bones Spring – shouting distance from the headwaters of the Walla Walla River – to its confluence with the Grande Ronde River at Troy. Nearly every wildlife species present in the Blue Mountains can be found including bighorn sheep, whitetail and mule deer, black bear, cougar, bobcat, coyote, timber wolf, and pine marten.

Three of my high school pals found evidence of "Bigfoot" in this expansive canyon country during the summer of 1982. A party of six anglers, including Paul Freeman, who reportedly had an earlier encounter with Bigfoot near Walla Walla, took a team of pack horses into the South Fork Wenaha where they found three different sets of huge, simian-type footprints. Plaster casts made from the sighting merely added to the brewing controversy over the presence of this mythical creature.

What's also unique about the Wenaha River watershed is bull trout – what locals call Dolly Varden or "Dollies." It's one of a few western rivers where populations are plentiful enough to allow for targeted catch and release. Back in 1950, newspaper columnist Vance Orchard, famous for his "Rambling the Blues" stories for the Walla Walla Union Bulletin, wrote about an early October hike he took into the upper Wenaha River watershed. The object of his quest was "whopping big Dolly Varden trout." Consistent with backpacking at the time, Orchard carried a canvas rucksack, fishing rod, and enough grub for an overnight stint. As it turned out, his quarry "had been up, spawned, and gone back downstream," according to a fellow angler who beat him to the punch. Regardless, Orchard and his buddy managed to catch enough trout for dinner and "for bragging."

When I was a youngster, it was common for anglers to camp at nearby Mottet Meadow and hike down into the South Fork of the Walla Walla River to fish "cutbait" for bull trout. I wrestled more than one such trophy from a log-lined pool, when angling with worms was legal. A memorable trip on the Umatilla River involved a small rainbow trout that I handed off to my small daughter, Diana, to reel in. She strained to make progress before saying, "It's snagged on something."

I took the rod back and felt the power of a large fish. "Looks like a big Dolly grabbed your little trout," I said. But before I could corral the fish, it coughed up its prey and swam to safety.

The first phase of my belated hike into the Wenaha River canyon with Ted and Ken involved a 4-hour drive from big sage country to a forested bench at 3,000-foot elevation, 25 miles east of Tollgate, Oregon. I was well familiar with the route, relying on an Oregon Gazetteer and a 1980 U.S. Forest Service map. In contrast, Ken monitored our progress with a hand-held GPS. We stayed on course until a "Road Closed" sign blocked access, but were soon on our way after conferring with a wildlife biologist who was hot on the trail of a wandering wolf.

With more than a little misgiving, I locked my truck and left it parked at the remote Hoodoo Ridge trailhead for the shuttle driver to find. Sometimes you have to live on faith. It was high noon and approaching 90 degrees in the shade when we shouldered packs. Standing on the canyon rim, we soaked in the steep side-slopes, rugged ridges and basalt outcroppings that rose to a plateau nearly 1,600 feet above the river. Three miles, six switchbacks, several piles of bear scat, and a quart of water apiece later, we swapped hiking boots for wading sandals to ford the river. Swift current surged thigh-deep to keep our attention, as did cobble slick from a summer's growth of algae.

Eager to wet our lines, we fished the north bank of the river downstream to Crooked Creek. I hooked and lost a decent-sized rainbow trout after swapping out a Renegade for a Stimulator for a Royal Coachman. Having intimate knowledge of patterns that attracted trout on the west side of the Blues provided little advantage over my fishing buddies. I wasn't frantic, but I couldn't help wonder where all the trout were. After all, these were wilderness waters and I was supposed to know what I was doing. Meanwhile, Ken caught two nice trout on a Parachute Adams and Ted enticed a 4-incher to an unnamed pattern that he tied himself.

Shortly after reaching our campsite at Crooked Creek, the first of two brief, yet violent thunderstorms reminded raingear was not on our list of items for the hike. Getting drenched was inconvenient, but not uncomfortable. "It felt more like a sauna than a cold shower," Ted said.

A second round of thunder and lightning rolled down the valley at dinnertime. The accompanying downpour put down the evening bite. Lacking a deck of cards and the option to stir hot coals because of a "No Burn" policy, we turned in shortly after dark settled in the canyon.

The first night produced no sweet dreams for me; rather a series of short naps interspersed with temporary changes in position. Waking to the sound of clanging pans, I reached for wading shorts that were still wet. On a positive note, clear skies beckoned. We fueled our minds and bodies with granola and a modern version of cowboy coffee that involved two motel packs of "Royal Cup" house blend placed in a one-quart aluminum coffee pot filled with river water and brought to a rapid boil.

The morning's fishing began at a promising stretch we noticed but skipped the day before. I soon tired of admiring Ted and Ken's casting and veered off on my own. A two-fly tandem, Bucktail Caddis and Copper John dropper, produced a cautious swipe from a large rainbow that refused to come back for a second pass. A Renegade fooled a 6-incher. Otherwise, action was slow.

With the sun directly overhead, I rested my backside on a massive log that could have been a telephone pole in another time and place and contemplated a change in tactics. A long, wide pool was formed where swift rapids sculpted a sandstone shelf smooth. I drifted a Beadhead Golden Stone through a deep slot and felt my line tighten to the pull of a foot-long rainbow that jumped 10 times. (I counted them for the record.) Two casts later, I hooked a large bull trout that pulled free when I worked it close for a photo. A 9-inch trout also came to the net. All three fish came from the heart of the pool, suggesting it's best to drift your fly deep if you want to catch more trout in the middle of the day.

I worked the nymph pattern downstream through a series of riffles, hoping to catch up with my companions. In this manner, I hooked and released several small trout and a 15-inch mountain whitefish. Coming around a bend in the stream, I found Ken squatted in the shallows, trying to scoop up small flying insects. "Some kind of mayfly," he said. "I think I have something close."

"How's Ted doing?" I asked.

"He's caught a few small ones," Ken replied. "I gave him two flies that produced for me, but rather than tie them on, he thanked me and put them in his fly box."

"In other words, don't give Ted your last good fly because it might go to waste?"

"In this case I didn't mind because I had several more."

I was reminded of the time I pointed out a likely fish-holding spot to Ted only to watch him cast in the opposite direction. Like Grandpa Harry once said, "You can lead a horse to water, but you can't make him drink."

It follows that some people have their own idea of what it takes to quench their thirst.

Because dinner plans that included pan-fried trout had been glossed over, it looked like canned sardines and Ritz crackers for supper until our combined efforts fooled three small trout near camp. With heads and tails removed, the trio of speckled beauties neatly fit a 6-inch diameter Boy Scout frying pan. Uncle Ben's pre-cooked wild rice steamed with reconstituted dried apricots completed the gourmet experience.

Rather than test the evening bite, we sipped Pendleton whiskey out of tin cups, ate handfuls of dark chocolate gorp, and watched bats chase bugs above the bunch-grass meadow. A brilliant cascade of stars emerged to remind how far from civilization we were.

You might think a person would sleep soundly after two days of hiking and fishing, but I got hot in my sleeping bag and slid off the pad before getting in one last nap to set me up for the day. Ted and Ken fared no better, as they reported fighting for position in their two-person tent. It was not that we woke up grumpy, but slow moving comes to mind.

Following another Spartan breakfast that reminded of the culinary limitations of meals during fire season, I climbed hand-over-hand up a hardscrabble slope to a perch located several hundred feet above the canyon floor. A warm updraft carried the sound of the river and jostled sun-dried stalks of balsamroot. Swallows swooped over sunlit basalt outcrops. The river flowed as if lacking a beginning or end. Morning shade slowly stripped away to reveal steep ridges, grassy slopes, rock outcroppings, and brush-lined ravines. Features that overwhelmed at stream level became larger pieces of the puzzle.

On the down-and-out hike to Troy, we stopped only to fish promising water within sight of the trail. Almost every deep pool with cover in the form of eddy flow or large wood held a bull trout, which were easy to spot because of their large size and clarity of the water. Getting them to take a fly, however, was a different matter. I caught up with Ken at lunchtime to find him crouched at the head of a long, deep pool with a serious look. "Had a bull trout," he shared.

Well, not quite, it seemed. As is the character of large bull trout, it had grabbed a small rainbow trout that Ken had hooked, holding on long enough to leave teeth marks. While I munched on a peanut butter sandwich, Ken switched to a Muddler Minnow, hoping for a rematch that did not happen.

The rest of the hike provided panoramic views of the river from afar. Our resolve was challenged though, when Ken's hand-held GPS indicated distance farther than shown on my dated U.S. Forest Service map. Nonetheless, we arrived at the trailhead to find my truck parked where it was supposed to be, complete with a welcome back note from the shuttle driver and complimentary candy bars. Unfortunately, the Troy convenience store was closed and we had to settle for the warm six-pack stashed in the backseat of my truck.

Our route home skirted the northwest boundary of the Wilderness Area on a series of winding 30-mile-per-hour gravel roads. Flocks of mountain bluebirds escorted from the summit of Mount Horrible, across the northwestern flanks of the Blues, and to the headwaters of the Tucannon River. I couldn't help reflect that, although much was discovered during the short hike and fish adventure, much more was left unexplored in a remote land that regional Indian tribes refer to as Spirit Mountain. While fish catching wasn't as good as I had imagined, there was satisfaction in finally completing my "spoke of the wheel" tour of trout streams whose apex originates from the Tollgate region of the Blues.

Wading Sticks

I'LL NEVER FORGET the hot summer afternoon when Grandpa Harry came staggering down the South Fork trail, blood streaming from a huge gash on his forehead. "I just lost a big trout," he blurted. "It took me downstream through a fast run, but got off when I slipped and hit my head on a boulder."

I was shocked at the time but the mishap shouldn't have been a big surprise. After all, Grandpa was getting on in his years. Five decades later, I know my strength and balance aren't what they used to be.

An earlier notable event occurred when Grandpa Harry waded across to where my older brothers had left me stranded and clasped my hand with the grip of a man who split six cords of wood every winter. Angling downstream to deflect thigh-high current that lifted me off my feet, he maneuvered us safely across to the other shore.

I eventually learned how to cross the South Fork without the assistance of Grandpa Harry's strong grip. And as things turned out, wading was useful for purposes other than for casting from either shoreline. For instance, wading helped me identify current seams and bottom features that dictated where trout lived. Even if my presence spooked my quarry, the forces and contours of the river were catalogued in my mind for use on a return visit. Equally important, wading got me to places where others didn't fish. It wasn't long before I waded with the best of them and had stories of big trout to share.

The South Fork of the Walla Walla River is the larger of two directional forks whose origin is near the summit of the Blues. It is a relatively docile stream, except during spring snowmelt, when it's prudent to remain on the trailside of the river. Once the river drops to fishable levels, you must approach deep holes and runs that form where swift current pushes against exposed bedrock from the proper side of the river. Overhanging brush, trees, and giant boulders create other situations that merit a precise angle of cast. Bringing trout to the fly on the South Fork involves having more than a passing interest in the sport. It requires thoughtful wading.

Don't get me wrong. I've experienced my fair share of midstream pirouettes and have slipped and fallen on my butt more times than I can count. More than one bonehead move has led to a water-filled vest or ball cap floating down the river. However, I quickly rationalize such incidents as *"no harm, no foul"* and push them out of my mind. You could liken my approach to wading to how I downhill ski. What counts is finishing the day standing up and in one piece. When it comes to wading, nobody in my family hands out style points.

All bravado aside, there comes a time in every stream fisherman's life where wading presents a challenge, as a recent experience with brother Dusty suggested. Things started innocently when he called to go fishing. I held my tongue when he apologized for short notice because I've spent much of my angling life catering to his personal agenda. Further discussion regarding my desires or schedule is generally not fruitful. I was nursing a torn ligament in my knee from a recent boating accident, but the football player in me said, "why not?" So I grabbed my gear and we headed for the South Fork. It would be just like the old days, us fishing side-by-side, seeing who could catch the most and the biggest trout.

My injured knee held up for the first few miles up the trail, creating a false sense of security. Brief climbs and low-gradient descents were handled with aplomb and the knee stiffened up only when I paused to rest. That was the good part. The bad part was my first venture into the river revealed a need for a supporting prosthetic device. Walking on loose cobble was like roller-skating on ball bearings. The shooting pain in my knee intensified each time I slipped or pushed off. The worst part was getting stuck in the middle of the river when my bad knee locked up and my good knee couldn't make up the difference. Consequently, I stood there like a dumb ass plotting a safe course to shore.

After that embarrassing incident, I skipped holes and deep runs if casting to them required wading. This conservative approach had its own set of hazards. I exposed my bare legs to stinging nettle and thorny blackberry. I got chased by a pack of bald-faced hornets hidden in streamside brush. These perils could have been avoided. To top it off, I stuck a favorite pattern on a log and left it dangling rather than test my wading skills.

Each concession to injury was both demeaning and frustrating.

Streamside maneuvers created another challenge. Steep drop-offs and fallen timber thwarted my bum knee. I longed for the strength and dexterity to jump over obstacles and bull through dense undergrowth. Instead, I was relegated to taking the long way around. Each detour cut into precious fishing time and restricted access to promising places where trout lived.

My challenging afternoon on the river nearly came to an abrupt climax when I slipped and fell on my backside while attempting to cross an ankle-deep riffle. From a position on the opposite shore, Dusty waved at me and smiled as I struggled to get up. He quickly shared that his balance was also "a little shaky." If that was his way of trying to commiserate, I didn't buy it.

I remember wondering why Dusty remained on the trailside of the river. It wasn't like him to give me first shot at good holes while he watched from the opposite bank. *That old dog is slowing down*, I thought. *But at six years my senior, he is a picture of what I will be, except his knee isn't as screwed up as mine.*

Water draining from my vest pockets, I found a friendly boulder to rest on and flashed back to my father-in-law's crazy ritual of crashing backwards into a Lazy Boy recliner when his leg strength waned and he could no longer flex his knees. I reflected on my beloved Brittany spaniel whose hind legs functioned as mere props after her hip joints wore out. Racehorses are put to pasture when their glory years are over. Punch drunk boxers greet customers at casino front doors. Aged baseball players sell insurance when they don't get picked up on waiver. The signs were there for me also. A trick knee that worked like a loose hinge when I put pressure was likely to shorten my angling career. *Are the days of hooking trout from locations accessible to only the strong and the bold behind me?* I thought. *Will I be relegated to casting to skittish trout from the wrong side of the river and competing for trailside space with my brother?* Clearly, a downhill pattern was emerging.

Several fly fisher pals rely on carbon fiber tubing wading sticks that can be folded up to fit in a holster or hung on a belt loop. Some wading sticks have contoured cork handles and rubber tips that grip between rock crevices for added stability. "Prevent a wading disaster," magazine advertisements say. You can spend up to $150 for such devices, although another friend brags about a ski pole he bought at the Goodwill store for a dollar.

You could say I ascribe to the Lee Wulff school of thought when it comes to wading staffs. "They detract from the free use of hands and arms, and that is a hindrance to wading," he wrote in an article published in *American Trout Fishing*.

Admittedly, I fell down on the St. Joe River while attempting to hopscotch over a gauntlet of shot rock basalt obscured by reed canary grass. I tossed my fly rod up the bank and crashed on my side, scraping my knee. My traveling companions were quick to remind that I would have been better served using a wading stick to probe for obstacles on uneven ground. I wrote the mishap off to a fluke. Later that same trip, while wading across a deep run, I slipped on moss-covered boulder and cooled off my privates. Although never in danger of drowning, a box of flies exited my vest pocket and floated out of sight.

Taking a hint from the angling history of Grandpa Harry, I combed a streamside thicket for a suitable wading stick. Hidden in a pile of driftwood was a well-seasoned alder branch that measured armpit high and broom handle thick. A roving beaver had chewed the tip down to a sharp point. Grasping the stick in my left hand and fly rod in my right, I secured position in the middle of the river and slapped the water with a series of one-arm casts reminiscent of my dearly departed brother, Daran. One difference is that my approach kept me upright in strong current, while he did the one-arm thing because he was too lazy to mend his line.

I eventually demonstrated my true wading potential and headed down the South Fork trail to meet up with Dusty. One fat breakfast trout flopped in the bottom of my creel. I vowed to restore strength and mobility to my ailing knee with regular stretching, rigorous exercise, and mega-doses of glucosamine. The message on the wall was clear, though. If I wanted to stay upright when chasing trout in moving water, I'd have to rely on a wading stick or chance taking an occasional header on a boulder.

HUCKLEBERRY LOVE

EARLY AUGUST in Blue Mountain country is best expressed as a morning spent picking high-elevation huckleberries followed by an afternoon of fly fishing. I partake regularly in both activities, starting back when tiny Mottett Creek was impounded to create mile-high Jubilee Lake back in the 1960s.

Jubilee Lake is the only game in town if you want to fish quiet water in the Tollgate region of the Blues. Because the small mountain lake freezes over each winter, it's primarily a put-and-take fishery for catchable-size rainbow trout. I start my day wading along the east shoreline while shadows are on the water. The bank drops off steeply with little room for a back cast unless you wish to tangle with a dense conifer over-story. Trout hang near shoreline points and underwater stumps and can be fooled with an Adams, Renegade or Blue Dun. The narrow inlet arm where Mottet Creek feeds cool water attracts bruiser-size trout that cruise the edge of bulrush looking for something larger than a scrawny mayfly. When the morning sun climbs high overhead and trout become wary, I work drop-offs opposite the main campground with a Beadhead Pheasant Tail or Prince Nymph. A Dark Caddis or Mosquito is often the ticket after sunset.

While trout fishing attracts me to the region, others confess to harboring greater love for the noble huckleberry. Unfortunately, some family members prefer to beg rather than labor by the side of a logging road in the hot summer sun. Consequently, and by partial way of illumination, I composed a short warning note after casual hints such as, "Looks like you scored a bumper crop." And, "Did you pick enough for me?" were tossed my way:

August 2012

Dear Siblings and Children,

There are two kinds of people in the world: those who pick huckleberries and those who eat huckleberries that others take the time and effort to harvest. In our family, a minority takes pride in belonging to the harvest group. This distinction has to do with their great love for the noble berry. Those family members who have more inclination to eat Mom's huckleberry cream pie than labor in the woods know who they are.

Yours truly,
DDD (Dad)

This candid aside serves as background to a trip that Nancy

and I took with my 88-year old mother. But before I get started, let me provide some perspective. It takes approximately 50 to 100 berries to fill the bottom of a 32-ounce coffee can. One quart of huckleberries an hour is a reasonable goal when you pick an average huckleberry patch in the Blue Mountains. While this rate isn't as bountiful as what might be gleaned from the slopes of Mount Adams, where huckleberries approach the size of a marble, it's decent enough to restrict roaming. Which reminds of a fishing guide who once told me, "Never leave fish to find fish."

The same advice goes for huckleberries. At least that's what I told Mom when she suggested we check out a nearby patch. She didn't argue when I refused, most likely because I drove and she didn't chip in for gas, although I'm guessing she had more to say on the topic. Some family members are better than others when it comes to keeping their mouths shut.

We picked our favorite patch for two hours before breaking for lunch. Mom relied on a walking stick to get back and forth, but did not complain, which is more than I can say for some huckleberry pickers – certain family members included. *One more quart of berries and I can wash the sweat off my legs in the cool water of Jubilee Lake*, I thought.

"Got to stay on task until we get another quart," I said to Nancy. She likens my relentless approach to foraging as one who hogs all the good trout holes, but I disagree. I am a consummate hunter-gatherer who appreciates Paleolithic fare and huckleberries are at the top of my list.

Nancy hung in there like a trooper, except when her internal GPS failed and she got lost. A pitiful cry, "I'm stuck!" echoed through the forest canopy and caused me to put my tuna sandwich down and look for her. A silver lining to the rescue operation was finding a patch of over-size huckleberries hidden deep in the shade of second-growth conifer.

I cringe at giving away more than a cup of huckleberries after navigating gut-busting U.S. Forest Service roads and eating the dust of fast-moving Ram trucks. Not to mention encounters with biting deer flies and thorny undergrowth. Worse yet is the sore back you get from stooping low. Which reminds me that Uncle Chuck once remarked, "Huckleberry picking is for women." In his defense, the remark was not entirely sexist. Without skipping a beat, he provided definitive male logic, "They're built lower to the ground than the average guy."

Well stated, or at least well understood. Mom is barely 5 feet tall and slowly declining in height to approach the crown of an average huckleberry bush. Nancy is 5 feet 4 inches tall, which allows her to stoop low. Sitting down on the job helps me alleviate back strain, as does picking uphill, but both options run out at some point. All I know is a day spent picking huckleberries requires this 6-footer (in cowboy boots anyway) to contort his lower back in ways that are not natural.

In my defense, I'm not a miser. I've been known to top up mom's harvest bucket with a handful of berries. I sprinkle liberal quantities of huckleberries on buttermilk pancakes for overnight guests. I'll even open a jar of Nancy's huckleberry jam to share with biscuits or toast. However, giving away a slice of huckleberry pie is a consideration only after its hiding place has been located.

I readily gift cherries and apricots from trees that grow alongside our home, but huckleberries are more precious. A friend once asked if I would consider trading a quart of huckleberries for two quarts of raspberries picked from his backyard patch. After an uncomfortable pause to consider my options, I invited him to accompany me for a day of huckleberry picking instead. That way he would have a better idea of his bargaining power if the topic came up again.

There is a long history of harvest in my family, whether for dry land wheat and irrigated alfalfa, in the case of Uncle Chuck, or stone fruit, as for Grandpa Harry. Pea harvest paid Dad's salary and put my siblings and I through college. As a youngster, I knelt on my knees to pick strawberries, transitioning to cherries and Italian plums when I got big enough to climb a ladder. Although meatloaf delight and ground beef casserole were on the family dinner menu more times than I care to remember, we never lacked for fruit pie at dessert time.

These things I mention to reinforce why I take great pride in gathering huckleberries. Finding a patch of this delicate fruit is like striking gold. The tiny purple berries are hoarded, protected, and parceled out with great reverence. Four cups dedicated to a pie is a splurge. A handful of berries sprinkled on Sunday morning pancakes borders on decadence. To stretch out her meager supply, Mom makes savory berry compote that is spread over creamy custard and topped with a deep layer of whipping cream. What sets this family classic apart from other holiday desserts is the intense flavor of wild huckleberries and her flaky pie crust.

After picking a self-imposed quota of huckleberries, I talk Mom and Nancy into letting me toss a fly on Jubilee Lake. The rise is on and I catch enough trout to supply fish for breakfast. The pleasure of harvesting huckleberries is in the knowing that an ample supply resides in your freezer for the year ahead. The pleasure of catching trout is in the knowing that they are there.

BURY ME with my fly rod

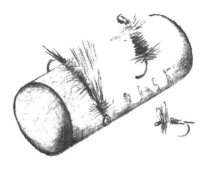

BACK TO LUGER SPRINGS

"ARE YOU SURE THIS IS THE PLACE?" Ken asked, reflecting on the broken-down picnic table and rusted fire ring napping in the shade of a pair of lightening-scarred ponderosa pine.

Although Luger Springs was 17 miles away from the closest paved road, finding the remote U.S. Forest Service campsite deserted on a blue sky Saturday morning in mid-August was surprising. *No matter; more fish for us*, I thought, as I turned my truck down a steep slope to where an old logging road cut obliquely into the steep hillside. A quarter-mile farther, the track widened to include a spur that allowed me to turn around between downed timber and several axle-busting boulders. I parked and we got out to peer over the edge of the road at a tiny ribbon of water far below. "There it is," I said to Ken. "That's

Lookingglass Creek."

Ken was silent. Up to then, he had no clue what he was in for other than a long drive on a series of winding back roads. In contrast, I had happy memories, though diluted by more than a handful of passing years. "My high-school buddies picked me up after I got off the night shift at the pea cannery," I said to Ken. "Bill and I rode up here in Norm's two-tone yellow-and-white '58 Chevy sedan. I stuck three bottles of Lucky Lager in my creel and hiked straight down this hill. We fished all day before climbing hand-over-hand back up the route we came down. Norm made it exciting on the return drive. He slid around hairpin corners, passed every vehicle we caught up with, and left a trail of dust in his wake."

By now Ken had time to ponder what the heck he had gotten into. Noting his hesitation, I spread my arms apart as if to absolve his fears and provided details on the day's plan. "We've got an easier route. This logging road stays several hundred feet above the creek where it follows power lines. We'll hike in a downstream direction for a mile or so then traverse the hillside to get to the bottom. The plan is to fish upstream to where the creek bends sharply to the west, climb a low bench, then follow a gentle grade back to the truck."

"This time I brought radios," Ken said, perhaps referring to the time we got separated on a previous fishing trip – something I had conveniently forgotten. Not to say he hadn't messed up at my expense at least once. Like when he led me through two miles of sagebrush in the wrong direction in search of an out-of-the-way still water venue. It wouldn't have been so bad, except that it was 95 degrees, we packed float tubes, and ticks were involved.

"Not a requirement," I explained. "We won't get out of each

others' sight. It's too small 'a water to split up. We'll have to leap-frog it."

With that brief introduction, we put our fly rods together and reduced essential equipment to a box of flies, spare tippet, and a bottle of water apiece. "I'm eating my lunch early," I said, chewing on a fried chicken leg and tossing the gristly bone into the brush.

"I'll eat my peanut butter sandwich later," Ken replied.

It had been 15 years since I last trekked into this same rugged terrain with my then college-age son, Matthew. The back half of our trip to Lookingglass Creek involved an overnight hike into the upper Walla Walla River. We skirted a scree-lined slope so steep it took us twice as long to hike out as the trip in. The rough path burned out a friend who never asked to go trout fishing with me again. Matthew and I camped where the trail crossed the upper South Fork and fished a unique place upstream of Skip Horton Creek near a place Grandpa Harry referred to as Box Canyon, where competing basalt layers pinch the river into a narrow impassable gap except during low flow. The experience was like going back in time. We cast into the head of giant bed-rock-lined pools and watched 16-inch trout rise eagerly to the fly. I have never since encountered so many consistently large trout that were not shy. The surprising part was when Matthew set his rod down after landing his largest fish and announced, "I'm done for the day."

"Are you kidding?" I said. "This is the best fishing I've ever seen."

"That's my point," he replied. "I can't imagine it getting any better."

I had been reminded of a return trip into Lookingglass Canyon when Nancy and I picked huckleberries on a nearby ridge.

The possibility had been on my bucket list, but a string of setbacks that included a torn ACL, prostate surgery, and a hernia operation set me back. What made me think I could still trek up and down this remote canyon like a billy goat? A lifetime of optimism, that's what! After all, a familiar face smiled back in the mirror whenever I brushed my teeth.

Ken is an accomplished fly tier and, like most having that inclination, is more than willing to share a pattern or two. This part of our relationship has taken on more importance after I lost the dexterity (and patience) to tie small patterns. Ken's reputation for trying to figure out what trout eat is widespread, as evidenced by a friend who once asked me if Ken "dove down to the bottom to look at things."

I replied, "He didn't have to because he brought out his stomach pump for the first few trout he caught."

In contrast to Ken's consummate approach to pattern selection, I select whatever fly I think will catch a fish, usually one of a dozen variations on the same theme. On a trip to the Walla Walla River, I started with a No. 10 Stimulator while Ken studied flying insects and tossed a variety of dries he thought looked similar. I'm not sure who I felt most sorry for, him for not hooking a fish or me for giving up several good holes only to have him come up empty. "They're looking for something big to eat," I finally said, handing him a Stimulator.

"I've got some flies like that," he said, hooking it to the wool patch on his vest.

I can summarize my thinking on pattern selection as somewhat similar to the novelist Thomas McGuane, who once described his favorite fly as: "When I look at it, I believe I'm going to catch a fish." Feeding Blue Mountain trout a steady diet of Renegades, Stimulators, PMDs, and Adams – simple patterns that rarely fail to entice trout – reinforces my belief.

Grasshoppers scattered to all points of the compass as Ken and I hiked down a little-used maintenance road that dropped in elevation to follow Lookingglass Creek's southward journey to the Grande Ronde River at Palmer Junction. When I was a youngster, we hunted grasshoppers for entertainment: long green ones, fat brown ones, yellow-winged, red-winged, and immature ones with stubby wings. To be a good grasshopper catcher, you had to be quick with your hands and pay attention to detail. You developed theories on where each kind of grasshopper lived and the best time to catch them. Those same lessons in habitat association applied to trout fishing.

The days of drifting a grasshopper through a deep hole with the aid of split shot were behind me, but the idea of tying on a Joe's Hopper came to mind. Meanwhile, Ken pointed out stray dickey birds, unique flowering plants, and the occasional animal scat. It's the wildlife biologist in him I've grown to appreciate. Twenty minutes of steady hiking later, we plunged down the steep side slope. Angle of repose challenged our descent as did slick mats of dead grass that hid pockets of loose shale. Zigzagging back and forth to reduce the strain on our weak knees, we navigated like novice skiers touring a black diamond slope with no way out except down.

After reaching the creek bottom, the situation became more complicated than it appeared from the ridge, which reinforced the notion that things often look better from a distance. Thickets of thorny buckbrush with an understory of stinging nettle prevented access to the stream. What followed were errant casts between overhanging branches and a decision to wade upstream in shock-cold water. This approach led to trading casts, gauging each other's tolerance for personal distance, and disturbing more trout than we caught. And the ones we caught were small. My expectations rose, however, when we arrived at a honey hole formed where flow dropped in elevation to crash along the face of exposed bedrock. "These big pools hold two or three nice trout," I said, sensitive to the fact we had come all this way and hadn't raised a fish over 8 inches long.

I gave Ken first crack at the pool. Surprisingly, he came up empty. About then, he declared, "My feet are frozen," and sat down on a narrow gravel bar to eat his lunch. When I approached the pool to try my luck, he pointed to the opposite bank where current curled over a large boulder. "Check out that big fish," he said.

"Uh oh," I replied. "It's a springer. I was hoping they would be gone by now. The problem with springers is they take over big holes. Their presence might explain why we're not seeing many trout."

When a second slab-sided Chinook salmon emerged from the shadows to join the party, I was reminded of a recent emergency rule posted by the Oregon Department of Fish and Wildlife that opened Lookingglass Creek to sport harvest of spring Chinook. I hadn't expected to find them this far upstream of the hatchery though. "They're paired up," I said excitedly. "It should be spawning time soon!"

The rest of the day played out like a G-rated Walt Disney matinee. We absorbed the tranquil setting and shared in the act of hooking and releasing wild rainbows. On occasion, my mind shifted into compound low and I sensed the strike of a trout before it showed. Other times I spooked one from the cover of shade or turbulent flow. These facts were committed to long-term memory. As wife Nancy once remarked, "You forget everything except every fish you ever caught." She is mostly correct.

Some things are easier to remember than others, particularly if you think the information will come in handy later.

Ken's patience paid off on the last long-lined pool of the day when he waded in below me to fool a fat speckled 11-incher that I missed from the head of the run. Our return hike up and out of the canyon was as easy as I remembered, except for brief encounters with patches of tick weed and wild rose. Slowly, yet surely, we traversed a sparsely wooded slope and ended up less than 50 yards from my truck. If Ken was impressed with my homing ability, he kept opinion to himself.

We loaded our gear, took one last look at the creek far below, and headed back the way we came. After cracking a second cold one, I passed a slow-moving fifth wheeler on U.S. Forest Service Road 63. Out of respect for my high-school buddies, Norm and Bill, I slid around the corner, sped into the next straightaway, and left the RV in a plume of dust – all the while ignoring Ken's white-knuckle grip on the grab handle above his window.

BURY ME with my fly rod

WATCHING YOUR HONEY CAST

MY BROTHER, DARAN, was a PGA professional who taught others how to enjoy the game of golf. He once posted an article on his website about the futility of trying to teach your "sweetie" how to play golf. He cautioned men golfers to remain patient and emphasized the importance of knowing their partner's motivation. "Leave the teaching to a professional," he wrote. "You'll come out ahead in the long run."

I wasn't smart enough to realize the same concept applied to me coaching Nancy on the stream. Blame my ignorance on a warm summer evening at the family cabin when the idea of an evening hatch worked its way into my brain and refused to leave.

The narrow shaded path to the Umatilla River from our cabin on Rock Creek Lane is lined with shoulder-high snowberry and an over-story of 100-foot-tall white fir. Needle duff cushions your step, song sparrows trill from hiding places in the brush, and the rumble of the river pulls you along. When the sun sank low and tree frogs began their two-part "rib-it" mating call, Nancy warmed to the idea of fishing. She grabbed her fly rod, tied on an obscure pattern that looked good to her, and headed to the river. I elected to relax on the side porch and give her some alone time.

Fifteen minutes later, I followed, but did not bring my rod. *I will sit on a rock and watch the action,* I promised myself.

"Any luck?" I asked Nancy, as I approached.

"I'm having babies hit it. Saw a nice one flip though."

A critical eye and an honest opinion can get you in trouble. In this case, I kept my thinking to myself. Nancy laid the fly out in short fluid casts that covered the water effectively when tree branches did not get in the way. I recalled an earlier occasion where I coached how to mend line to ensure that her fly drifted naturally in the current. As I recall, the evening went downhill from there.

Nancy doesn't like anyone telling her what to do. I sense it has something to do with her childhood. Blame it on the way she was raised. Either that or it's in her genes. Whatever the reason, it's a fact. I can't tell you how many times I've heard her say, "Don't tell me what to do."

I know this, but after 40-plus years of marriage I can't help offering advice when we are on the stream. Like when I observe several bad casts in a row. Or when she throws to the wrong spot or the same spot too long (*either approach is a waste of time*). It's not like I say, "Don't do this," or "Don't do that," or "What the heck are you thinking?" I try to be diplomatic. More like, "Have you tried the head of the pool?" Or, "It looks good below that big rock."

Of course none of these ploys work to my advantage because Nancy sees right through me. It's almost as if she knows I'm going to go there sooner or later and waits to catch me in the act of "telling."

While sitting on a comfortable rock trying to mind my own business, I noticed that Nancy lost track of her fly. More than once she failed to set the hook when her cream-colored No. 14 PMD slipped below the surface and a trout flashed next to it. *There we go, another missed strike*, I thought. *A trout pretty much needs to swallow the fly before some people notice.*

About then, Nancy hooked a chunky 8-incher, laughing as she reeled it in. "Look! There's another trout chasing it!" she yelled.

After reeling in her third small trout of the evening, Nancy sensed my eagerness for a try at the rod. Admittedly, I secretly hoped to get in a cast (or 2 or 3 or 12) after she had her fill. I've never been good at pretending otherwise. However, I didn't want to "horn in" on her spot or take a fish she might otherwise catch. I have yet to feel remorse though after I pull one out from a place she can't reach or fails to recognize as good holding water.

Things eventually worked in my favor and my patience was rewarded. Nancy stepped back from the cobble shoreline, pointed her rod in my direction, and asked if I wanted to have a go at it. "Sure, thanks," I replied, trying to hide my eagerness.

That's when she pulled the rod back and said, "Forget it. Go get your own rod if you want to fish."

You'd think I could take what I gave out on a regular basis, but it's not so easy when the shoe is on the other foot. The truth was I badly wanted to catch a fish after sitting a spell, watching trout chase Nancy's fly, and trying to keep my mouth shut, although not always successful at the latter.

"Anyone who wanders over to the river without a fly rod is not very smart," Nancy said with a Cheshire cat grin. "You don't need to be such a bad sport though. I was only joking. Go try a few casts. I'm done for now. But remember that I'm the only one who would give up my rod to let you have a try."

Fair enough, I thought. *Lesson learned.* I grabbed her fly rod before she changed her mind and worked my way to a side pool where she had neglected to place a fly. Three casts later I was fast into a 6-incher that jumped twice before it tossed the hook.

Herding Trout

Fishing dogs come in all sizes, shapes, and colors. Most are in the faithful companion category; grateful for whatever attention that you might provide. On the flip side, they will roll in rotting salmon carcasses and experience chance encounters with skunks, porcupines, and cockleburs. In contrast to humans, however, dogs quickly rebound from a bad day on the water. They forgive and forget because all they really want is love. A pat on the head is accepted as if it's a special gift.

My first dog was a border collie mix who bonded to me after following my brother, Daran, home. Daran always kept something to eat in his pockets. If there's one thing that dogs understand, it's food. Soon after he moved in, Dagwood found a place to sleep at the foot of my bed. He was a lover, a fighter, a car chaser, and a moocher, but he protected me from strangers until my early teens when he was run over by a moving van. Most tire-biting car chasers didn't live half as long.

Next up on the roster of family canines was a puppy that Nancy and I adopted from an animal shelter shortly after we married. The dachshund part of Pappy's heritage was confirmed by the obvious identity of his mother. A black tongue, curly tail, and rough coat indicated his estranged father had been a roving chow. Pappy's handful of tricks included chasing his tail, shaking hands, and dancing (i.e., standing on his hind legs while I held his front paws and led him around the room). He would also lie down and roll over on command. When I said, "Hey, Pappy, wanna go fishing?" he would spin around and yip like a coyote.

What followed after Pappy passed into the light was a string of large field dogs, including Brittany and cocker spaniels, and a Labrador retriever. Their collective temperaments ranged from sneaky smart to friendly dumb. Some were excellent pets and others were more trouble than they were worth. All reached the age of weak bladders, gray muzzles, and cataracts that clouded their vision. After enduring several years of male territorial behavior and large amounts of pet waste in the backyard, we settled on a small-bodied female Corgi. They are of the herding dog variety, genetically tuned to nip at the heels of stubborn calves and sheep. Imagine a big dog attitude without all the baggage. Short legs, an alert bark, and a big heart go along with the package. Keeping with family tradition, Lucy loves to go fishing.

Lucy does not stand up on the bow of my boat, point her nose into the wind, and wait for the strike of a salmon. The sound and vibration of an outboard engine unsettles her. Another drawback to a mariner lifestyle relates back to when we fished on the Yakima River. I pulled up the boat anchor to move to another catfish hole when Lucy grabbed the chunk of herring I had left on a 2/0 hook and began choke it down. My loud "NO!" was ignored as she clamped onto the bait tighter than a pair of vise grips. It took Nancy's help to peel Lucy's snarling lips apart and work the hook loose. Needless to say, that was Lucy's last fishing trip on the boat.

Corgis are also noted for having a keen sense of smell. As testimony, Lucy senses the opening of a can of tuna two rooms away. The faintest hint of residual fish slime left on your hands keeps her attention for days. However, it's neither the taste nor smell of fish that attracts her when we are on the stream, but the chance of grabbing something that moves. The sight of someone leading a trout to shore is to Lucy like a ball of twine is to a Siamese cat. Lucy may be of a herding breed, but she goes on point when it comes to the splash of a trout – whether on the end of your line or taking a mayfly from the water's surface.

What's odd about Lucy's attraction to stream trout is she avoids a lawn wet with dew. She refuses to leave the shelter of the front porch when it's raining and avoids the neighbor's sprinklers like the plague. But she will wade into moving water up to her chest and pose vigil for a chance to nip at a trout on the end of your line.

On a recent trip to the Umatilla River, Lucy followed close at my heels. I caught and released two small trout, being careful to unhook and drop them into the shallows away from her snapping jaws. The third trout was not so lucky because of my ill-timed toss. Lucy grabbed the small fish from the shallows before it could right itself and swim away. I commanded in a guttural tone, "Drop the fish!" She clenched her jaws down tight, bared her teeth, and growled, as if to say, ""It's mine and I ain't letting go!"

I dropped my rod and tried to force Lucy's jaws apart, but she gave another warning growl and held onto her prize. The tail of the small trout hung out of her mouth.

Based on the previous experience with Lucy and catfish bait, I knew there was no way she would give up that fish. Then a thought came to me like a face card that covered an inside straight. I shoved her head underwater and held it there until she was forced to come up for air. And the ploy worked. Lucy came up gasping for breath and the trout wriggled free.

"I hope you grow up to be a 12-incher," I said as the trout took off like a rocket, apparently no worse for wear.

By now, Nancy had arrived at my side. "That was mean," she said.

"You're right," I replied. "I should give Lucy a treat."

It just so happened that I had a spare Oreo in my shirt pocket. Sometimes you need a quick sugar fix. Instead of the usual last bite though, I gave Lucy the entire cookie. And as near as I could tell, the treat mitigated for her dunking.

The next morning, Lucy trotted eagerly alongside when we walked the shaded path to the river. I took position on the cobble shoreline and made a few false casts. She waded into the shallows up to her chest, scanned the water for the telltale splash of a trout, and prepared to herd it to shore

I guess that's why I'm a dog person. Dogs rarely hold a grudge. A cat would have avoided me for a month.

Big Four

I WAS 10 MINUTES LATE for an early morning rendez-vous with Ken after stopping at Starbucks and getting stuck in a lineup of latte lovers. *Why don't coffee shops have a self-serve station for patrons who want a tall cup of coffee, black?* I thought. *I'd gladly pay extra than wait for fussy patrons whose morning cup of Joe involves a five-part recipe.*

To make up for my tardiness, I stopped at the hometown Spudnut shop for a sack of glazed donuts. Donuts buy forgive-ness. You can be late if you bring donuts. More important, do-nuts allow you to stay on task without experiencing the inevita-ble late-morning crash in blood sugar that occurs after you eat a bowl of Wheaties and run out the door. Ken employs a different strategy to start his day. "One bowl of cereal isn't enough," he says. "I'll eat two different kinds."

Ken and I were on our way to a small "fly fishing only" lake located deep in the Tucannon River watershed. The early season adventure was spurred by an email from a friend who fished there when high winds and snow were in effect. Mark reported catching eight trout before retreating to the comfort of his truck to avoid hypothermia. "I took most of them on a Hare's Ear," he wrote. "The copper thread imitates air bubbles trapped on the abdomen of caddisfly and mayfly pupae."

"I think catching hatchery trout has more to do with motion and contrast," I fired back. "They react to something that hits the surface with a splash. Or they are attracted to the reflection of Flashabou tinsel or a gold beadhead in sunlight. There's also the hatchery pellet theory. Small brown flies usually work. Especially around normal feeding time at the hatchery."

Mark did not reply, which suggested that sharing cynical thought kills meaningful discourse.

Ken and I had plenty to talk about on the hour-and-a-half drive to Big Four Lake, beginning with a report of an angler who bragged that he caught trout on sixteen straight casts using a Green Maribou Leech. Unfortunately, he only had one fly of that size and color, so others settled for catching a fish every once in a while. One of his buddies went back three days later with a handful of Green Maribou Leeches and did not entice a single trout. "We decided to go to Deer Lake, where fish had been stocked the day before," he said. "They bit on anything that fell from the sky."

The program at our most recent fly club meeting was another topic of interest. Pictures of a fancy lodge in Patagonia, spectacular landscapes, and hero shots of huge trout carried the hour-long presentation. "I wonder how much dinero went down on that trip," I said to Ken.

"He said the lodge and guides cost five thousand per week," Ken replied. "Then there was airfare and a tip."

"He had to tip for the lodge?"

"Yup. 10 percent on top of everything else to be divvied up among the staff."

"I don't think I could justify the cost to Nancy," I said. "Her way of getting even for me going on an expensive fishing trip is buying jewelry."

In the time it took to travel 30 miles down Highway 240, we had denigrated angling for trophy fish and justified our quest for hatchery trout. After all, giant rainbows from Patagonia are just stockers of a different time and place.

We motored through sleepy downtown Dayton and turned due east on a secondary road to follow the course of Pattit Creek. A line-up of wind turbines perched on a nearby ridge provided an industrial look, suggesting a different scenario than what the Lewis and Clark Expedition experienced when they passed the same route two centuries ago. Asphalt pavement turned to gravel as we approached Hartsock Grade. I mentioned a bear sighting from the year before. "You only see them when you're not looking for them," Ken replied.

Still, I couldn't help look. Five doe grazed on a side slope sprinkled with balsamroot in full bloom. A hen turkey pecked the ground near the cover of a lone ponderosa pine. The narrow gravel road dropped steeply into a canyon where the Tucannon River ran low with an emerald-green cast. A winding river road led us upstream and past familiar landmarks: the Last Resort, Washington Department of Fish and Wildlife hatchery complex, and a roadside impoundment where anglers plunked Powerbait from the comfort of folding lawn chairs.

Fording the upper Tucannon River to get to Big Four is a challenge when flows are charged with snowmelt. I was reminded of an earlier trip when a member of our party revealed a physical impairment that did not become evident until he stepped off the bank into ankle-deep water and fell on his backside. "Do you have a bad knee?" I asked, gently helping him to his feet.

"I have two bad knees," he replied.

Having a member of your party swept downstream is not an ideal way to begin a fishing trip. The crossing involved stringing a rope across the river and strategically positioning two of us beside the challenged individual.

Flows were more moderate when Ken and I arrived, and we easily found a safe route to cross. I threaded my way through dense willow to reach the backside of the lake and tied on a Zug Bug. *The splash of my cast and sunlight glinting off the gold beadhead would surely attract*, I thought. Ken, on week three of recovery from a rebuilt right thumb, stationed himself on the tip of a narrow peninsula that split the small lake in half. After doing his best imitation of a broken wing cast for 15 minutes, he announced, "I think they're taking emergers."

"I might guess the same," I replied, "Except without a single take, I don't have a clue."

Ken is member of a fly fishing religion known as "match the hatch." In contrast, I try not to waste time trying to understand what hatchery trout are thinking. My standard approach involves changing patterns until I hook a fish and staying with that fly until it fails to attract another fish or is lost in a tree.

No takes led to boredom and boredom led to me tying on a No. 14 Renegade and dragging it past a school of redside shiners that gathered at my feet. Two casts later, as a light breeze stirred the service, I hooked and landed a trout. In the space of 5 minutes, I went from managing daydreams to being on point. *Had I found the secret fly?* I wondered. *Was I now a fly fisher?*

Another half hour passed without a strike, so I swapped out my sink tip to a floating line. Meanwhile, Ken tired of casting left-handed and switched to a Red Chironomid suspended below a strike indicator. The change in tactics led to him catching two trout while sitting down with an open bottle of Sam Adams ale in his lap. "I pumped their guts but couldn't find anything," he yelled my direction.

That's when I noticed twenty or so trout milling in a corner of the lake where cattail crowded the bank. Several fish faced my direction as if waiting for a handful of hatchery pellets. They scattered, however, when I cast their direction. *Something has to work*, I thought, so I tied on a No. 12 Adams, a universal pattern that rarely fails to entice a strike. Several casts later, when a slight breeze ruffled the water's surface, I hooked a nice trout. Two casts later, I hooked another. Then a half dozen strikes in a row. *Had I found the secret fly? Was I now a fly fisher?*

Most trout are indiscriminate about what they eat. Cut open a stomach and you'll find sticks, bits of plant material, insect parts, Styrofoam, pebbles, etc. Pretty much any item deposited on the bottom, suspended in the water column, or floating on the surface is fair game to a trout. According to a study by Finnish scientists, brown trout grown in a hatchery environment have a greater tendency than wild trout to grab at any food supply they see. Only after hatchery trout habituate to a water body do they recognize food, actively search for it, and become selective. Whether Big Four trout had reached that level of understanding was debatable.

The rest of my day was dedicated to fabrication of angling theory. Consider that some strikes coincided with a gust of wind that ruffled the water's surface. Others came in bunches, when a patch of biters suddenly arrived on the scene. Several trout broke the surface as if pouncing on a terrestrial. A few nipped at imaginary mayflies. Ken claimed to have enticed a rise as a result of increased stealth. During one stretch, he hooked five trout in a row. "What's going on?" I yelled. "Looks like you found the secret fly."

"I saw a trout chasing a shiner," he said, "So I put on a silver-headed Wooly Bugger. They seem to like it. Want one?"

My yield after fifty casts with his fly totaled one trout. Meanwhile, the bite went off for Ken. *So much for the shiner theory and my quest to fool Big Four hatchery trout*, I thought. *Then again, it's possible the guy with the magic Green Maribou Leech left them with sore mouths.*

Stocker Trout and Dogs that Eat Celery

Any email message that starts off with, "One of our trees fell on your cabin," gets your attention. I'd been eyeballing the neighbor-to-the-north's 100-foot high, insect-damaged fir tree for over a year – ever since its twin deadheaded and fell across our back lot. The first rotten fir took down a lengthy portion of cyclone fence and missed my toolshed by an arm's length. Standing dead trees are great if you favor downy woodpeckers, but not so much if they lean precipitously over your beloved cabin. Picture files attached to Leonard's email somewhat eased my angst. Other than a crumpled ridge cap and several dents along the drip edge, damage to our cabin's roof was minimal. I considered myself lucky, compared to another cabin neighbor who had to replace several trusses when a novice tree cutter dropped a large fir tree on his roof.

Our circa 1940 rustic log cabin nests in the middle of the Bar M Ranch, a former stagecoach stop, hot springs resort, and dude ranch located alongside the upper Umatilla River. Three generations of family owned and operated the ranch for over six decades before they sold it in 2003 to an entrepreneur business-man who ran the operation without profit, but got his money back by logging old growth timber on the property. The ranch was sold a decade later to a conservative church group that my mother refers to as "the Baptists."

I spent a late November weekend pounding the cabin's dam-aged roof metal smooth, splitting wood, and smoking up a batch of salmon. Multitasking is something I've honed to a fine art. Time passed pleasantly. Moonlit hours were spent writing in my journal and taking a hot soak in my cattle tub spa. I also went trout fishing. Not in the river (the season closed October 31), but in a one-acre pond located a short stroll from our cabin's front stoop. The Bar M pond was stocked with foot-long rainbows in early summer. They had gained inches and were as fat as pigs from a steady diet of hatchery pellets. Walking down Rock Creek Lane that cool November evening led me to wonder if they were rising. The sun had disappeared below the south ridge and a stiff cold breeze blew up-canyon, scattering dried cottonwood leaves and rustling stalks of cattail that lined the edge of the pond. A trail of wood smoke from a neighbor's chimney hinted that win-ter would soon be here.

I strolled over to the pond and studied the water surface, searching for a dimple, splash, or swirl – anything to suggest trout feeding activity. A small bat swooped silently over my head. Then another. *That's a good sign that bugs are flying,* I thought. In my right hand, I held Nancy's fly rod. The seldom-used five-weight rod she left leaned up in the corner of the cabin's master bedroom. A scruffy looking No. 12 Parachute Adams was tied to a short section of leader riddled with wind knots.

I stood between two beached canoes, faced downwind and slapped the water with her fly. Seeing a swirl, I cast to it and felt a grab. This same outcome was repeated for four consecutive casts: solid tugs felt on the drop or during a slow strip, each time without achieving a hookset. I examined the fly in rapidly fading light. *What? The hook has a busted tip!* I searched my fly box for a Brown Wooly Bugger or other proven "hatchery pellet" pattern and consummated a knot with shaky hands. Two casts later, I'm into a fat rainbow trout. I worked along the shoreline until I could no longer see my rod tip, hooking and landing six more large trout. Whether because of an evening rise, random feeding, or instinct triggered by feeding time at the hatchery, the result was a welcome, late-season trout fix.

The following morning takes me along a series of gravel byways that spur off Spring Hollow Road and north to the town of Weston where I grew up. Back roads. Nancy doesn't believe in dillydallying on the way home. I have a different philosophy. You never know where a detour will take you. I don't glean a box of apples from trees beside the road or fill the bed of my truck with black topsoil dug from the edge of a rancher's wheat field (both activities have served me well in the past), electing instead to stretch out the two-hour drive home with a visit to a long-time friend.

Back in the day, Lars and I bombed minnows in the creek that ran behind his house, hypnotized barnyard chickens, and built campfires to fry slabs of bacon that we ate between slices of flame-toasted Wonder Bread. We later cruised back roads in his right-hand-drive Austin Healey and vintage VW bug. Nowadays we're more likely to talk about universal topics such as climate change, politics, or the latest obituary notice.

I pull into a large turn-around gravel driveway that fronts a clapboard sided two-story house, park behind a vintage Nissan pickup, and am greeted by typical farmyard sights. A small donkey brays from the shelter of its paddock. Two free-range roosters cackle and strut, sporting resplendent grizzly hackles. *Think of all the Adams I could tie with those!* Loose tin on the barn roof flaps in the morning breeze. A two-tone Chevrolet sedan, Ford Explorer jacked up on two wheels, and small travel trailer complete the scene. I get out of my truck and navigate a broken concrete sidewalk framed by assorted garden equipment.

Lars's wife, Fran, spots me through the front window and waves hello. I climb the front porch steps and enter the living room. A big brown boxer stares at me as if I was a pot roast and he hadn't been fed in a month. All four bony legs twitch in cautious tension; his saggy jowls tighten; and he emits a low, steady growl.

"I don't know what's wrong with Tiger," Fran says with a bemused smile, as if their "child" greets every other guest with a wriggle of his hind end and a sloppy kiss. I stand still as a post and let Tiger approach. He woofs nervously and backs off as if to say, "Screw you and the horse you rode in on." When I offer my hand cautiously for a sniff, he looks to the side and growls.

"Go get in your box," Fran commands in a guttural tone after which Tiger retreats to a large travel crate placed in the doorway to the kitchen. "He's usually not like this," she says.

""I pulled a rack of salmon out of the smoker when I left the cabin a half an hour ago," I said. "Maybe he doesn't like the smell."

Known to form a deep attachment with their owners, boxers are an intelligent, loyal breed of canine. I want Tiger to like me, but my presence appears to have made him anxious. A bad first impression can be difficult to overcome, but I'll try.

I remember dealing with aggressive dogs as a youngster when I delivered the daily news. You stand still, let them sniff the air, and watch their body language. Tail down and ears up indicate aggression. A wagging tail with ears flattened signals interest. Let them smell you. Don't make abrupt motions that might alarm them. Keeping a treat in your back pocket to share shows that you are their best friend. Despite my judicious training, a hostile German shorthair bit me once. He was chained to a clothesline and I underestimated how far he could run toward me without choking himself. That might explain why I don't trust long-legged, slick-hair, twitchy dog breeds to this day.

My attention diverts back to Tiger when he wanders from the comfort of his crate to check me out again. It is obvious my presence makes him uncomfortable. We are even on that account because his erratic behavior makes me uneasy. I find a step stool to sit on, which encourages Tiger to lower his head, and stick a wet nose in my crotch. I don't mind a dog getting in a good sniff, but I draw the line when they nuzzle my privates, as if desperate for their mama's long-lost teat. I lift Tiger's head away from the source of his attraction, but he refuses to back off. That leads to a standoff, where we stare at each other – eyeball-to-eyeball – from a distance of less than a foot. My testosterone level rises. And at my age, that is not always a good thing. Thankfully, Fran intercedes, "Tiger. Stop it!"

Lars shuffles his feet. "Why don't we give him some celery," he says, matter-of-factly. "That might settle him down."

Fran grabs a stalk of the green stuff from the refrigerator and hands it to me. Tiger's ears perk up in a good way. His stub of a tail wriggles and his ears lower. I hold the celery in my right hand while he gnaws on it like a tasty rib bone. A stray celery leaf, followed by a string of drool, drops on my leather boot. I pet Tiger's head and scratch him behind the ears while he nuzzles my shoulder and dives into my crotch with his big square head. He licks my face. He tries to crawl in my lap. He looks soulfully into my eyes. We are now the "bestest" of friends.

I sense that Tiger is willing to sleep at the foot of my bed, follow me to the end of the earth, and defend me from all intruders. I don't, however, plan to pursue our relationship further. He is not only high-strung, but he is high maintenance. Any dog that growls until you offer a stick of celery is not my idea of an ideal companion. I'd almost rather another tree fell on my cabin than take him fishing.

One quart per hour is a decent gathering rate for huckleberries in the Tollgate region of the Blue Mountains.

Secret Family Recipes

PAN-FRIED RAINBOW TROUT

Use your heirloom Barlow or recently-purchased CRKT pocketknife to make an incision in the belly of a small trout (8- to 10-inchers are best) from the anal vent to the isthmus. If you don't know what the isthmus or anal vent is, read a copy of my book, *Fishes of the Columbia Basin.* It devotes an entire chapter to fish parts. Remove the gills and guts of the trout and use your thumbnail to scrape the kidney loose from the backbone. Pat the fish dry using a paper towel and dust it lightly in flour. Salt and pepper the body cavity. Add bacon grease or butter to a cast iron frying pan and fry the fish over medium heat, turning once. The eyeballs turn white, skin is crisp and brown, and the meat peels easily from the backbone when trout are perfectly cooked. Serve with bacon, one large egg fried or scrambled, and hash brown potatoes. Alternatively, serve up bacon, egg and fish and follow the delectable trio with dollar pancakes soaked in butter and maple syrup.

MOM'S HUCKLEBERRY CREAM PIE

Start by making a 9-inch pie shell. Put in mixing bowl 1½ cups all-purpose flour and ½ tsp salt. Cut in ¾ cup vegetable shortening. Use your fingers to lightly blend the mixture, but don't knead the dough as you would for biscuits. (I once did that and had to feed the result to the birds.) Add ¼ to 1/3-cup ice water until pie dough forms a ball. Roll the dough evenly with quick light strokes until it's about 1/8 inch thick and line the pie pan with the crust. Press a fluted edge using your fingers and prick the bottom and sides with a fork. Bake the prepared crust at 450 degrees for 12 minutes or until lightly browned.

The cream filling is next. Place into the top of a double boiler 1 cup of granulated sugar, ½ cup flour, and ¼ tsp salt. Mix. Stir in 3 cups milk and cook for 15 min over hot water, stirring constantly until the mixture thickens. Add three egg yolks, slightly beaten. Cook for 3 minutes, add 2 tbsp butter, and cool. Add 1 tsp vanilla and set aside.

The huckleberry topping starts with 1 cup of sugar, 3 tbsp cornstarch, ¼ tsp salt, and ¾ cup water that you stir over low heat until it thickens. Add 2 cups huckleberries, stir, and heat until the huckleberries incorporate or "juice up." Refrigerate the topping until it cools.

You are now ready to build the pie. Spoon the cooled cream filling into the pie shell and refrigerate until it sets. Spoon a layer of cooled huckleberry topping over the cream filling and refrigerate the mixture. Finish the pie with a layer of whipped cream (not Cool Whip). The result is a decadent dessert that you don't pass out freely to anyone under the age of 10 unless they help pick the berries. Offer close friends and family members the smallest slice possible with a promise of another only after everyone else has had a portion.

Dick Ecker and his favorite two-hander work a stretch of the
Hanford Reach, Columbia River shoreline on a cool fall day.

Part Two. Chasing the Elusive Steelhead

Fly Fishing, by its very nature, is not a sedentary
preoccupation, nor should it be pursued by
apathetic subscribers

-Don Roberts

BURY ME with my fly rod

Little Purple Fly

My first steelhead on a fly took place on a blue-sky, autumn afternoon on the Hanford Reach of the Columbia River. Until that indelible day, the occasional trade-off of spinning with fly gear had merely reinforced the notion that playing both sides against the middle rarely gets you what you want.

The 50-mile long Hanford Reach is the longest non-impounded stretch of the Columbia River upstream of Bonneville Dam in the continental United States. Another way of saying it is the "Reach," as known to locals, retains the characteristics of a natural river. With an average discharge of 120,000 cubic feet per second and widths that span a half-mile in places, reading the water can be daunting. Big rivers can be broken down into habitat features that make sense, however. Hanford Reach steelhead hold in long runs where the main channel is braided by cobble islands, alongside washtub size boulders, and near shoreline kick points sculpted by Ice Age floods. Identify these locations and you will find steelhead.

My fish-catching ability did not suffer when I switched from spin casting to tossing flies for rainbow trout in Blue Mountain streams. Indeed, early forays with garden hackle taught me how to read the water and bring feisty trout to the creel. However, a major challenge to upping the ante for steelhead was lack of proper equipment. Casting into the wide expanse of the Columbia River with a hand-me-down Wonder Rod felt inadequate. Meanwhile I had learned how to catch steelhead using a wide repertoire of spinners. There is rarely impetus to initiate new methods when old ones serve your purpose.

There came a day though, when watching fly casters ply their skill led me to purchase a 7-weight Cortland rod suitable for swinging flies in big water. My new outfit came out of the gear closet only sparingly, however, because I lacked the work ethic to stay with what it took to bring a steelhead to the fly. You could say I needed a well-directed nudge. That's where "Dr. Bill," as affectionately known to friends, came in. Twenty years my senior, Bill was the ideal mentor. "Worst thing is we'll spend a nice day on the river," he said, when we finalized plans.

Although the upper Columbia River was closed to sport harvest of steelhead at the time, local angling regulations allowed for catch and release. A large number of summer-run fish had returned to the Reach, attracting anglers from all across the state. Addicted fly fishermen set up camp in the Russian olive grove adjacent to the Ringold Springs shoreline, some for several weeks at a time. Opportunity appeared ripe for me to try my luck with a fly rod.

Bill motored his aged Dodge pickup under the speed limit for the entire 40-mile drive to the Ringold Springs hatchery complex. His relaxed pace only heightened my anticipation. We turned off Road 64, took in a view of Rattlesnake Mountain, crossed a large irrigation return canal south of a set of rearing ponds, and drove a half-mile on a narrow gravel road to Parking Lot 7. A worn trail led to the river through an abandoned field of knee-high cheatgrass. Tall willow and cottonwood flushed with gold fronted the high water mark. Wood smoke, curling from the metal chimney of a nearby farmhouse, suggested an early frost.

My cleated boots crunched the shells of Asiatic clams that lay scattered along the cobble shoreline. Coots bobbed and milled offshore. A copse of honey locust stood sentinel above an abandoned concrete weir. Washtub-sized boulders, scattered in a checkerboard-like pattern, created a long stretch of broken water. Farther downstream, a narrow gravel bar extended into the river. Bill stopped well short of the water's edge to describe where we would be fishing.

Reaching into his top vest pocket, he handed me a small fly. It was a simple pattern: dark purple hackle tied ahead of a twist of white rabbit hair, black yarn body, and gold beadhead. I tried to hide my surprise. The fly appeared more suitable as a dropper for rainbows under an Elk Hair Caddis than swinging for steelhead. To my knowledge, classic northwest steelhead flies were large, streamer-type patterns having vibrant color and wrapped with Mylar piping or Crystal Flash. I came prepared to fish with several such flies tied up for the occasion.

Noting my dubious look, Bill assured me that the little purple fly was a good choice; "Here's a black-hackle variety if you don't like purple, but steelhead don't care. You can always try one of yours if you want."

I went along with what Bill suggested, thinking the added weight of a bead would help position the fly near the bottom and that sunlight shining off gold might attract. Besides, what did I know? Bill had caught plenty of steelhead on flies and I didn't have a single notch on my gun.

Anxious to get started, I tied the little purple fly on my tippet. Bill pointed me upstream. His two-piece rod remained broken down and held loosely in the crook of his right arm. "Why don't you try the head of the drift," he said, pretending to fumble with his gear. "I'll slip in behind you after you work downstream a bit."

Without a moment's hesitation, I waded in ankle-deep and cast to where current broke over the inside edge of a washtub-size boulder, relying on my trout-catching instincts to identify places where a steelhead might rest. I mended my line, let the little purple fly swing across the current and imagined how it looked to a waiting fish. There was a feeling of harmony with the river. *Why did I wait so long to test my mettle*, I wondered?

It didn't take long for me to get into a steady rhythm of casting and retrieving. When Bill moved in upstream, I waded to reach the heart of the drift. We worked slowly downstream in unison until I felt a quick tug. Retrieving slack, I found a small steelhead dancing on the end of my line. The drag on my reel screamed as line sliced across the current with intention. A flash of silver showed where current broke over a narrow rock ledge. *So this is what it feels like to hook a steelhead on a fly*, I thought. Never did I feel in control though, having had my heart broken too many times in the past.

Following a second acrobatic leap, the battle proceeded back-and-forth in small increments until the small steelhead turned on its side and I eased it into shallow water for release.

Nested in the corner of its mouth was Bill's little purple fly, the gold beadhead shining like an LED. I remember thinking, *how could something that seemed so unattainable be so easy at the moment of triumph?*

Ten minutes later, Bill hooked a steelhead of his own. I watched him lead the fish to shore for release before we walked upstream to repeat the drill. My mood was post-coital. I inhaled the musky odor of damp cobble and admired sage-studded hills that glowed in the flat light. When the tympanic "garoo-ah-ah" of a southbound flock of sandhill cranes got my attention, I turned to the sky. The brief moment of revelry was interrupted, however, by another tug when my fly drifted downstream to where divergent current back-eddied to create a foam line.

Once again, the battle was on. Twisting, leaping, taking line from my reel – the steelhead eventually tired and came obediently to shore. My second steelhead on a fly was a virtual twin of the first: 5 pounds or so, a silver bright hen, freckled across the back and caudal fin, cheeks blushed candy-apple red. After she regained her breath, I pointed her back to where she came from with the brash confidence of someone who embraced the craft.

Later that same afternoon Bill drove to the Ringold Springs shoreline where half a dozen anglers lined up downstream of the hatchery outlet creek. "Steelhead lay next to that rock." Bill said, pointing to a large boulder two strides from the river's edge. "There is plenty of room to cast below that guy in the green jacket if you hurry."

The body yarn of my little purple fly had now frayed to create a bolder more attractive silhouette – or so I imagined. I grabbed my rod and trotted downstream, where I hooked and landed two more steelhead "next to that rock." The guy in the green jacket turned out to be our friend, Dick, who has never forgiven me for stepping in below. I could not have scripted the four-fish day any better.

As for the fact I may have low-holed Dick, I can argue that I was naïve about fly fisher etiquette at the time. Blame my oversight on first-time exuberance and that little purple fly – a simple, yet effective, pattern whose moniker remains etched in stone as the "Dr. Bill."

Two-Handed Loaner

Waiting in the Deschutes Canyon fly shop for our shuttle driver to arrive, I sorted through a rack of waders, enticed by a sign on the front door that said, "All items 25% off." Admittedly, my interest had more to do with elevating status among my peers than personal need. Problem was I thought the hand-written tag next to the waders read "$145" when the price was "$445." "A little rich for my blood," I muttered to nobody in particular.

"But they have a zipper." Dick said, when I made a face and replaced them on the rack. "For easy access when you have to relieve yourself."

"How 'bout I pay myself a buck every time I drop the suspenders on a pair of $89 waders instead?" I replied.

The last 100 miles of the Deschutes River's northward path

to the Columbia River was designated Wild & Scenic in 1988. Boater access is restricted on some segments of the river during peak-use periods. In addition, motorboats are only allowed upstream to Mack's Canyon (river mile 23.9) on alternate weekends from June 15 to September 30. A primitive trail for hikers and mountain bikers leads upstream from the Deschutes State Park along the old railroad bed. Dozens of campsites, a few with pit toilets, can be found along the entire river corridor.

The idea for a float trip for summer steelhead on the lower Deschutes sprang from an email exchange initiated by Mark. "I had a great trip on the Deschutes; nine fish hooked, five landed (if you count the one released from 5 feet away)."

Irrespective of how you choose to measure success, Mark's invitation served as the ideal entree for my first steelhead trip on the Deschutes. He had fished the iconic river for several decades, was an experienced boater, and regularly improved his game at regional fly casting clinics. His role as trip organizer seemed well suited for someone known to be meticulous at his job.

Our buddy and coworker, Dick, signed up "purely for the fishing." Dick's casting talent had been developed from a beachside dock in Sequim Bay during countless work lunch hours and, later, on Olympic Peninsula streams. His standard approach was to play the role of the tall quiet type unless confronted with B.S. Otherwise, whatever events transpired over the course of the trip were fine by him.

Then, there was me. Someone with a self-centered personality that could test the patience of others. I complained about the late-season campfire ban. I had opinion on the menu and sleeping arrangements. I wanted to know how many hours would be devoted to fishing versus floating.

As the early October date drew near, Mark emailed a description of fly patterns he planned to bring. "I will tie the Green Butt Lum Plum, Engagement, Streetwalker, Princeton Tiger, and a few others to share. Dr. Bills might work too. I caught steelhead on a purple fly two years ago."

A follow up email from Mark attached a detailed list of nutrition-balanced menu items along with his rationale for our daily allocation of beer, wine, coffee, and water. Also included was an item-by-item list of personal clothing, bedding, rain gear, and fishing equipment. One last bit of information related to a U.S. Bureau of Land Management requirement to pack human waste out in a portable toilet, otherwise known as a honey bucket. "A word of warning," Mark wrote, "We will camp where there is good fishing, not where there is an outhouse."

The most exciting news was Mark's offer to lend me a 7-weight Spey rod. Ever since I visited Scotland, I had dreamed of testing my skill at two-handed casting. Both Dick and Mark promised to give me a lesson in the art.

The kidney-jarring shuttle ride to Macks Canyon took place on a 15 mile-per-hour dirt road. Smoke from a recent range fire lingered at the launch. Everything was copacetic until gear was safely stowed in Mark's experienced ClackaCraft and he scoffed at my roe-stained chest waders. "I'm not sure I want you in my boat, " he said.

"It's my badge of shame," was the best I could come up with.

The first day's float took all of 5 minutes – hardly enough time to soak up the spectacular canyon scenery. We beached on a sandy beach at Friday Night Camp and staked individual tents at the edge of a wide flat filled with rabbitbrush in full bloom. I took careful note of railroad tracks far enough away from camp that trains would not disturb my sleep in the night.

A competitive moment with another angler arose shortly after I hiked upstream. "Who's that?" a startled voice bellowed, as I forced myself through a narrow stand of willow. I showed my face to assuage his fear over a grizzly bear attack, we chatted amicably, and I moved upstream to dab a weighted nymph in a series of pocket pools. Meanwhile, my two companions worked boulder-studded water downstream of camp. I couldn't help notice that their casting distance was twice what I managed with my one-hand Cortland.

Lunch gave us time to catch up and swap stories. I munched on a tortilla chicken wrap while Mark described a steelhead he hooked ("I saw it jump"). Dick shared that he had a grab in the same location. My only action was from a foot-long northern pikeminnow – a fact I did not share.

"Look for current that is walking speed," a friend had shared. After a short nap, I headed downstream to survey the river for slicks, seams, and boulders that might provide steelhead respite from swift current. Unfortunately, my mind worked overtime without reimbursement. *Is floating line deterrent to getting a fly down to where a steelhead might pause? Casting for Deschutes River trout is a waste of time in the middle of the day. Does the same behavior hold true for steelhead? Should I swap out my monofilament leader for fluorocarbon? They say it is less visible on bright days.* Unfortunately, an analytical mind can suffer with absence of data.

Tired of battling a stiff upstream breeze, I returned to find my tent lying on its side, rocking back-and-forth on its fiberglass frame. Mark stood stoic over a Weber grill that flared up like a Texas oilrig. "Never done that before," he said, before switching to a backup camp stove to prepare dinner.

I sat in a canvas camp chair and listened to water cascading over smooth stone. Exposed basalt glowed like burnished bronze in the setting sun. A squadron of rock doves flew by in tight formation. Short-bodied October caddis, wings as large as big Stones, hovered clumsily over streamside alder. The rumble of a passing freight train gathered force and dissipated over open ground.

Mark confessed to puncturing his waders during an encounter with a patch of blackberries. The recollection caused him to pour wine into his tin cup with vengeance. Mark and Dick voted to set the alarm for 5:30 a.m. I voted to rely on my pineal gland to arouse me at the first hint of dawn. I did not fret my minority position once crickets sang me to sleep.

I slipped into "a dream inside of a dream" state of mind, something that occurs when I transfer seamlessly from one dream to another without waking up. It doesn't happen often, but when it does, I have twice as much to think about when I really wake up. As I recall, neither part of the two-act play involved naked women, getting lost, or struggling against a team of highly trained assassins. Muddled events and suppressed desires aside, dawn came early. I contemplated aching bowels when light from Mark's lantern flooded the sitting area, blaming my discomfort on cheap wine and rare steak. "I need to catch a fish today," Dick said when he emerged from his tent hacking mucous from a chest cold.

Milky Way skies had turned cloudy overnight to moderate the normal downward plunge in the early dawn temperature. We skipped the scheduled breakfast of reconstituted scrambled eggs and bacon crumbles to get on the water before other anglers. Fueled by a three-day old blueberry scone, I headed upriver with resolve, while Dick and Mark returned to their "hot spot" downstream of camp. The trail to the top of the alder grove was damp from rain and dimpled with boot prints. I picked my way past rocks crusted with lichen and inhaled the acrid fragrance of big sage. A drift boat slipped by in low light, unsettling a belted kingfisher perched on a shoreline snag.

I had the stretch to myself, or so I thought, until a beaver flushed from the shallows. His dark head appeared as a smooth boulder in low light, close enough for me to reach out and touch his paddle tail. Finally sensing my presence, he submerged and swam past, trailing a stream of bubbles.

"Let's catch a steelie," I told myself. But I didn't.

We broke camp to begin the second day's float. Although Dick's confidence was wavering, he regrouped to razz Mark. "You would make a good guide. You've got all the skills. Business would be great for a month or so. At least until your clients found out you couldn't get them a fish."

Sensing pressure to deliver the goods to a pair of discouraged fishing partners, Mark piloted past Nooky Rock, Bull Run, and Fall Canyon, stopping only where ample shoreline allowed us to spread out. Meanwhile, my blood sugar plummeted. It seemed like hours before Mark declared camp where streamside alder had been burned down to smooth stumps. *Reminder: stash a granola bar in your waders when someone else is in charge of mealtime.*

It was here, at a desolate location we called, "Camp Armageddon," where Mark gave me my first casting lesson with a Spey rod. Unfortunately, I was not familiar with the lingo. Introductory terms as shooting head, anchor, and D-loop came across as a crash course in a foreign language. Consequently, I struggled to relate to his patient instructions. It was embarrassing, but no more so than failing to master a dance step that required three moves. "I'll lend you one of my casting videos when we get back," Mark said, before leaving me to my own devices.

Dick was equally kind about my shortcomings with the long rod. "You're not doing bad," he said, shortly after I confused the Snap T with the sign of Zorro.

Feeling more confident with each cast, I worked a promising stretch with a desolate landscape at my back. I swung my fly across deep pocket water; a shallow riffle; and a long, slow run. I focused on short, accurate casts, using my left hand as a fulcrum and not rising on my toes when I went top hand. One thing in my favor was staying on the same side of the river. Consequently, there was no confusion about which arm to put in motion, except when a sudden gust of wind threw me off balance, in which case I had to start all over again.

Dick called it a day and returned to camp after a party of recreational rafters low-holed his position. Exploring on my own now, I detected an offshore boil that suggested a large boulder lurking below the surface. I was intrigued, having caught steelhead in proximity to similar features in other rivers. The boulder was at the absolute limit of my casting ability though, and overhanging alder lurked behind. Thinking this is where having a Spey rod comes in handy, I waded to my waist and delivered a purple Dr. Bill with my best roll cast. Three tries later, as the fly swung seductively across the downstream edge of the boil, I felt a sharp tug, followed by a head-shaking pull. *Fish on!* A small steelhead came to the surface, while I frantically loosened a too-tight drag to stretch out a short but spirited fight. Eventually, the fish turned on its side and I backed up to lead it to shore. That's when an extra four feet of rod, a steep bank, and dense shoreline vegetation challenged me. Luckily, the small hatchery hen was hooked solidly in the corner of her jaw. I slipped her onto the bank and pounced like a pit bull after fresh meat.

My heart raced as I held the struggling fish with trembling

hands. After not hooking a steelhead in over six months, I would have lit up a Camel to smooth things out – if only I smoked.

"One thing is for sure," I said to Dick when I returned to camp to show off my catch, "I couldn't have delivered a Dr. Bill to that submerged rock with a one-hander. My back cast was too restricted with alders."

Rather than congratulate my good fortune, Mark raised an eyebrow. "Why did you keep it?" he asked.

"I thought we agreed to keep the first hatchery steelhead that one of us caught for dinner," I replied, looking to Dick for affirmation.

"That was the plan," Dick said. "Let's barbecue it tonight. I'm not up for another rendition of chicken wrap."

After devouring a pair of orange-meat filets poached in a bed of onion and lemon slices, we huddled in a makeshift shelter to hide from a stiff west wind with a bite to it. Mark and Dick showed little interest in another recap of my epic battle and I sensed where they stood on broader matters, such as social equality for the masses. So I retreated to my sleeping bag, after which the pitter-patter of rain on the tent roof lulled me to sleep. Skies were clear when I got up to pee, revealing a celestial show as spectacular as that witnessed when I chased redsides in the upper canyon in June.

Dawn broke to reveal dark clouds gathering from the west. Several crows glided silently past the camp. A four-pack of speeding mergansers followed, wing patches flashing like a NASCAR checkered flag. Dick poured himself a cup of coffee, made a nest in the back corner of our three-sided shelter, and hacked mucous. The morning air smelled like a campfire recently doused.

There was no loitering after breakfast dishes were cleared. We stowed the honey bucket, packed camping gear, and said goodbye to Camp Armageddon while leaden skies drizzled. Running out of river miles now, we beached the drift boat in an open campsite near river mile 7. In anticipation of high winds, we secured the corners of our tents with the biggest rocks we could find.

After a brief refresher lesson in the art, I perfected the Circle Spey Cast, which, as near as I could tell, consisted of picking my line out of the water, letting wind blow it upstream, and slinging it forward with a two-hand twisting motion. Dick cautioned, "Don't hook yourself in the eye," before he moved a safe distance away to toss his Purple Avenger at least 30 feet past my best cast.

Dinner conversation revolved around Mark's most recent battle with a steelhead. "Does getting it within 10 feet of the bank count as a catch?" he asked.

I wasted no time in replying, "Nope. A volitional release at 10 feet is still a lost fish."

Dick also showed lack of empathy. "Sorry, you have to land them if you expect to take credit for a catch."

The truth was, Dick and I were envious. Hooking a steelhead demonstrates proficiency in reading the water and placement of fly, even if the outcome doesn't end up on your catch card. The remaining evening's entertainment consisted of drinking box wine ("Bandit" as I recall. I can't recommend it) and watching the adjacent group of campers pop off target shots across the river.

I hid in my sleeping bag when the warm glow of Mark's wake-up lantern illuminated the wall of my tent, reminded that among family members I'm known as the early bird, but not so with fishing buddies. With ball cap secured, I crawled out ready for one last October morning of steelhead fishing.

A slow-moving stretch of water downstream of camp yielded one good tug, *but was it a cautious take from a steelhead or a nudge from a resident redside trout?* All I could do was speculate and hope for another chance. While my Spey technique improved, I often messed up anchor placement and struggled to lay out my line smoothly. More than once, I forgot I held a two-handed rod and flailed away with a one-handed toss. Regardless, I learned more about fishing for steelhead than I knew coming in.

Any shortcomings in my substance and style were forgotten after Mark let me prepare the first genuine camp breakfast of the trip: Jimmy Dean sausage patties, fry bread with raspberry jam, and Del Monte "Lite" pears. I sat next to the river and ate from a tin plate while bank swallows dive-bombed caddisflies that formed a cloud over frothing rapids.

We broke camp at mid-morning, leapfrogging past a steady stream of rafters over the last seven miles of float. While Dick and I soaked up the sun, Mark rowed skillfully past Gordon Ridge, Colorado, and Rattlesnake, and Moody rapids; each with their own set of challenges. Bank anglers who hiked up from the Columbia River confluence cast spinners and worked side-planers along the shore. Lining a broad sandy beach at the Deschutes Park take-out was a flotilla of jet boats, outboard pleasure craft, and rubber rafts. Big-bellied swimmers of both genders, dogs chasing Frisbees, and small children with pails and shovels greeted us. While we unloaded equipment, a fish checker approached to ask: "How'd you do?"

"It wasn't red hot," Mark replied, "but we managed to catch two steelhead."

I bit my tongue. His account of the trip was a reasonable rendition of the facts. Plus, there remained a remote possibility I might get invited for a return trip if I kept my mouth shut for once.

Praying for Steelhead

"I NEVER DID FIGURE OUT what made you decide to attend the final church service," my older sister, Darcy, said, buckling up in the back seat of my truck where our Corgi had laid earlier in the day. Corgis have a double coat of hair; the outer layer is constantly getting turned over. *Darcy's dark gray wool coat will attract dog hair like a magnet,* I thought. *I hope she won't notice until later.*

"I look at it as an adventure," I replied. "The Weston Methodist Church was an important part of our life growing up. I guess I'm nostalgic about tradition."

A high school friend and local historian, Sheldon, had posted a recent notice on his Facebook page that informed the Weston Methodist Church was "down to five members" and that the last service, "A Benediction to 140 years," would be held at 6 p.m. on December 23. Along with readings from scripture and the usual holiday songs, a presentation on the history of the church was planned. Attending an evening service was inconvenient, however, because Weston was a two-hour drive from the Tri-Cities and I don't like driving in the dark. I finally settled on spending the night with Mom in Walla Walla where we would celebrate Christmas Eve the next day. Kill two birds with one stone, so to speak.

In front of us was a white-knuckle trek over 4 inches of snow and ice to the town where Darcy and I grew up. Nancy was in her usual anxious mode when road conditions challenged, but otherwise assumed the role of a willing companion to my version of an adventure. I tried to talk Mom into going along but she said, "I don't feel the need after playing the organ there every Sunday for 40 years."

I'd rarely attended a church of any faith since my college days, except for weddings and funerals. Back in the day, Mom and Dad, without fail, marched us five Dauble children up the hill to the Weston Methodist Church every Sunday. I received my first bible after taking communion alongside adult members a day short of my tenth birthday. As a teenager, I read and studied the Old and New Testaments and earned the coveted Boy Scout "God and Country" award. You could say I was an indentured servant to the Protestant faith – a prisoner of the Methodist religion. I put in enough pew time to know who nodded off during the sermon, trimmed their fingernails at communion, peeked during the invocation, and sang out of tune. Despite this judicious upbringing, and like others who leave the fold to fish in lieu of attending their church of choice, I tired of eating gospel pie and drifted away from organized religion.

We three arrive ahead of schedule and find downtown Weston lit up for the holidays. Festive stars hang from streetlamps and multi-colored lights adorn the windows of the town library. I turn up icy Main Street, pass the Blue Mountain Tavern and other two-story brick buildings that have been closed for years, and climb the steep hill to where a familiar whitewashed building welcomes. Leaning concrete steps lead us up to the belfry steeple and through double doors to the main area of worship, where a crowd of 20 or so adult parishioners, several young children, and a small choir are in attendance. The minister stands at the pulpit reading a letter written by a senior pastor who chose to celebrate the poignant occasion from afar.

While we search for a place to sit, a thoughtful attendant chases us down with a bright yellow program. A folded insert has an Advent song printed on one side and a lengthy email text from the Reverend J. Quinton Kimbrow with the subject line: "A few thoughts on Weston," printed on the back. A quick glance of scheduled activities indicates that we have missed two "warm up" hymns, including a favorite holiday tune: #246, "Joy to the World."

"So much for arriving early," I mumble to Nancy. *That dang Sheldon*, I think. *I twice asked him when the service started and both times he replied, "6 p.m." Evidently, historians have a different sense of time.* Meanwhile, Sheldon sits serenely behind the minister, attired in a long flowing white robe that exposes brown wool socks and Birkenstocks. I forgive him for his transgression, because forgiving is sublime.

Upgrades to the church interior since my last visit a decade or so ago include red velour cushions that grace seven rows of hard mahogany pews, a broken piece of stained glass replaced, and new wool carpet leading to the main pulpit. Missing is the familiar scene of Mom at the Hammond organ, friends and neighbors who have long since entered the pearly gates, and a passing of the silver collection plate for which I had specifically set aside $20 as atonement for past and future sins.

Fortunately, pew time allows ample occasion for daydreaming. I reflect on the long list of miracles attributed to Jesus and let my mind drift back to when I cast a hand-tied Gray Hackle in local streams and prayed for a keeper-size trout to show. And, back to the Sunday morning when, at age 16, I placed a wrinkled greenback in the collection plate and prayed to catch a steelhead. "Father, bless this home for it is ours" and "Lay me down to rest" once rolled off my tongue as quick as the ABCs. Early religious training required memorization of passages from the back of the hymnal and demonstration of fluency in New Testament verse. These faith-abiding behaviors were firmly ingrained in my persona. Praying for that first steelhead was merely a natural extension of my early upbringing conveniently applied to another avocation that requires a great deal of faith.

Bringing myself back to the present, I'd like to say that my singing is confident and on key, but *thou shalt not bear false witness*. Nancy's soprano voice pretty much carries each tune while Darcy and I mumble and look around with great earnest as if to catch a glimpse of the Holy Spirit. Following three inspirational prayers, two scripture readings, four unfamiliar hymns, 23 hand-written notes read from the Blessing Box (note: our late arrival negated the opportunity to enter a blessing), a rousing group "Hallelujah," and a lengthy historical narrative that Sheldon delivers, the finish line arrives and we all clasp hands for the benediction. Sadly, not a single hymn in the updated songbook ended with a perfunctory "Amen." Evidently, the "so be it" part of the Methodist religion, one I often relied on for moral support after an unsuccessful day of fishing, is no longer in force.

Some things never change though. Following the challenging hour-and-a half-long service, cookies, coffee, and small talk awaited in the daylight basement. And as near as I can tell, my bank account of faith remained in the black – despite all those Sunday mornings I skipped church to chase steelhead.

BURY ME with my fly rod

Secret of Maribou Run

I WOKE UP IN THE MIDDLE of the night trying to sort out what I did wrong. *How did I miss that steelhead in the middle of Maribou Run? Was it bad timing or poor technique? You only get so many chances! I'm positive I felt a pickup earlier though, in the place where Dick hooked his steelhead. Then again, maybe I dragged my fly across a rock and a steelhead moved in after I left.*

When I met up with Dick and his cousin, Terry, at Ringold Springs the previous morning, Dick said, "Haven't touched a fish in two days. Let's go someplace else."

That someplace turned out to be a remote stretch of Columbia River shoreline that local fly fishermen call Maribou Run. I once took flack for disclosing its location in a magazine article. Although specific details were not provided, an accompanying photo of a solitary angler with a distinctive tree on the opposite shore was a dead giveaway. The friend in the photo told me later, "Don't ever use a picture of me again." Another angler sent me an uncomplimentary letter, accusing me of "ruining the fishery for all."

I don't share their concern. Every shoreline point, rock pile, and gravel bar in the Hanford Reach present a likely holding place for summer-run steelhead. Dozens of such locations are scattered throughout 50 miles or more of shoreline. It's just that some locations provide convenient access to bank anglers, while boaters favor others. As my ex-school teacher wife, Nancy, states whenever the topic of so-called secret fishing locations comes up, "A secret is not a secret if more than one person knows about it."

After arriving at Maribou Run, Dick and I gave Terry first shot at the best water. He hadn't caught a steelhead on a fly before and we wanted to further his enthusiasm for the sport. I started a punt of a football upstream while Dick took position in a nearby stretch of frog water. "You'll get hung up with a bead-head," Dick said, when I offered one to Terry as a gesture of friendship. Never one to heed advice when I have opinion, I tied the rejected fly on my tippet.

The distance between Dick and I increased exponentially. Longer casts, coupled with a methodical rate of retrieval led to his slower pace. Another factor was my desire to get to the honey hole. When Terry cut his "beat" short, I delivered a token cast to a drop-off where I once caught a steelhead, reeled in, and walked down the bank to a large boulder that marked the best part of the run. Meanwhile, Dick hadn't moved more than 10 feet. *We'll be here in the dark at the rate Dick is fishing*, I thought, as I eased into position. Two casts later, my line tightened on the swing. I raised my rod butt in response, but it was too little, too late. *A pickup and I missed it.* I cast to the same spot. *Nothing.* I waded thigh deep, laid my line out farther, and repeated the drill. *Nothing.* My awareness remained elevated as I methodically worked the remainder of the run.

An hour of concentrating wore me out, so I took off my chest pack and rested on a friendly clump of reed canary grass. Meanwhile, Terry had moved upstream of Dick. "Oh!" he exclaimed.

"Oh what?" Dick said. "Was that your drag going off?"

"Yup."

"You had a steelhead."

Could just as easy been a rock, I thought. *Still, it's better to keep your companion's hopes up.*

The water level continued to drop, revealing the tops of boulders and providing clues where steelies might lie. Sunlight peeked from behind giant cumulus clouds to provide a false sense of warmth. When a stiff northeast breeze came up to compromise casting, I lost interest. It appeared to be too much work with too little reward.

I stood up and brushed a crust of algae from the backside of my waders, reflecting how Dick had admonished me for having mud on them. "I bet you scrub yours clean with a toothbrush every night before you go to bed," I replied.

We like to get each other's goat, but Dick is more effective at getting mine if prompting a rebuttal is what counts. In other words, he's better at keeping his mouth shut when I spout off. The other part of it is my screw-ups. Like the time a lens popped out of my cheap Polaroid sunglasses and floated out of sight. I had to squint "one-eyed" the rest of the day. Or when my reel fell off on the first cast. Another time, in a moment of inattention, I slammed my truck's hard tonneau cover on his Spey rod. Luckily, he had a spare.

"You sure are slow," I said to Dick. "No wonder bait fishermen low ball you. You stay in one place too long."

"One cast, three steps," he replied.

"I lined you up with a locust tree on the other side of the river and you haven't moved in over ten minutes."

"Sure I have."

One thing I've learned is that acquired skill only comes with dedication and practice. Long, smooth languid casts; left hand resting on hip; rod held low in right hand, as if he had little else to do. Dick's relaxed pose reminds of an artist at his easel. In contrast, my style resembles a house painter slopping primer on lawn furniture. Dick eventually worked his way to the sweet spot and placed his fly several feet past my best cast. By now I had quit counting his footsteps. The sun lingered on the horizon, my position was comfortable, and it was pleasant to sit and critique.

About then Dick raised his rod tip. "Might be a bass," he said, stripping in slack. "Either that or a small steelhead." Sure enough, a silvery form broke the surface and took off fast enough to make his reel sing.

"That's a noisy clicker!" I yelled.

Compared to the smooth purr of my well-oiled Gunnison 5 Ross reel, the drag on Dick's Hardy Perfect reminded me of glasspacks speeding around a corner. Then again, I may have been sensitive to him hooking a steelhead in a place where I had tried and failed. What some people consider noise is sweet music to others.

"I'll catch one in front of you (again) one of these days," I wrote to Dick in an email as reminder of a day where I had outfished him.

"Getting a fish in front of me is no feat," he wrote back. "It's when you get one behind me that you have something to brag about."

"Agreed, although it would be tough for me to catch a fish after you slap the water and chase them away. Not to mention I get sufficiently bored fishing behind you that I'd have to hang myself from the nearest cottonwood."

"Maybe you should slow down and catch more fish."

Introspection and self-examination are words rarely used outside of consultation with a shrink. But like my mom used to say on days when she sensed my feelings had been badly bruised, "Time heals all wounds."

BURY ME with my fly rod

DECIPHERING SCAT

I HADN'T DEVOTED MUCH THOUGHT to what beavers might leave in their wake until Ken pointed out something that resembled an abandoned Cuban cigar. We were hiking along a stand of brush willow that bordered the Columbia River near Ringold Springs. "Hmm, wonder what this is from?" Ken said, pushing at a small brown object with the toe of his wading boot. Ken's inquisitive mind thrives on the unusual. Consequently, things that attract his attention more often than not compromise time that could be spent fishing. As partial explanation, our respective expertise lies within specific areas of training (his is wildlife, mine is fisheries). There is sufficient overlap in the two disciplines to ensure that certain objects of nature have shared interest. In other words, there is ample opportunity to both learn from and confuse each other.

The small animal product appeared much smaller than what a 120-pound Labrador retriever might deposit on and was impregnated with tiny bits of what looked like dried berries. I replied, "Maybe a coyote?"

"I don't think so," Ken said. "Ever seen beaver scat?"

"Can't say as I have," I replied.

"*It* looks like little Pres-to-Logs."

His description reminded me that dried animal dung serves as an important source of dry fuel in third-world countries. *Pres-to-Logs, huh?* All this time I figured the stack of artificial firewood in front of Safeway was constructed from sawdust and glue when the odds were good it was amended with animal manure. I was not offended, however, having grown up around cow pies and horse biscuits.

I occasionally look at animal scat when I'm hiking in the woods or walking along a stream. To be specific, I "look" at *it* as opposed to "looking for" *it*. I choose to refer to *it* as scat, rather than the more pejorative doo doo, poop, crap, feces, excrement or shiza because I have a PhD in the biological sciences. Having an advanced degree allows you to drop scientific-sounding words into cocktail party conversation with little fear of reprisal.

Rodents, ungulates and lagomorphs produce vegetation-based droppings that can be safely scrutinized. Raccoon scat has also been known to get my attention. In contrast, I have little interest in poking at what roving black bears leave behind. Everyone has a limit.

I may be one of a handful of individuals aware that suckers align their fecal pellets along the bottom of rivers and streams, a phenomenon that relates to the concept of positive rheotaxis, or how fish generally face upstream in the current. The finding came early in my scientific career when I studied the feeding ecology of suckers. Fish versions of *it* largely go unnoticed, mainly because nobody wants to acknowledge that fish poop in their drinking water.

With a fair piece left in the hike before Ken and I planned to swing a fly for steelhead, my mind began to unload idle thoughts. One such thought concerned an obscure scientific paper that described algal growth being elevated near active beaver lodges. The author concluded the effect was the result of nutrient loading from beaver feces. Feces is a commonly used scientific term, confusing in the sense *it* can be either singular or plural.

By now, I couldn't help but look down at the ground for more of *it,* which isn't the same as looking into the contents of a one-hole outhouse. Believe me, there is a huge difference between casual observation and obsessive behavior.

Wouldn't you know? The more you look the more you see! Scattered about the shoreline were similar specimens of native ordure. Bending down for closer examination of menu items for one of nature's engineers yielded fresh insight. "I see tiny bits of wood in this one," I yelled to Ken, who, after nearly taking a header on slick cobble, was momentarily deterred from looking for more *it.*

On further observation, the small Pres-to-Log-like deposit was determined to be genuine beaver scat. This conclusion was reinforced by a series of distinctive five-toe tracks and a tail-drag that led from the river to a thicket of coyote willow.

"Do you have a camera?" Ken asked. "I'd like a picture."

"Are you serious," I replied. "A picture of beaver scat?"

"Yes. I need one for my collection."

"How many pictures are in your collection?"

"Over 15 different animals. The file on my computer is called 'the shitz.'"

Keeping an open mind, I arranged the best-looking beaver product on a flat rock and took several photos, including one with a dime next to it for reference. I am obligated to say that there is a huge difference between "best-looking" and "pretty" when it comes to describing *it* though. Esthetics come into play more than you might think.

Before I could put my camera away, Ken bent over and gently teased the object of interest apart with a small stick. "Take another picture, would you?" he asked. "To show what *it* is made of."

Why not? I thought. *After all, fishing doesn't have to be all about catching fish.*

CAR BODY BEACH

ONCE AGAIN, I meet up with fishing buddy Ken for a day of casting at the elusive steelhead. Ken is late, but I don't mind because Eric Clapton is jamming on satellite radio with Delaney and Bonnie and Friends. *They don't make eleven-minute-long songs like that anymore,* I think, as I check the Columbia River discharge at Priest Rapids Dam on my iPhone. The U.S. Geological Services graph shows flows dropped overnight from a high of 190,000 cubic foot per second to 60,000 cubic feet per second. Based on an estimated eight-hour lag for reduced flow to reach our fishing location, conditions should be ideal.

Our route northward on Road 68 takes us past cultivated circles of alfalfa and corn, feedlots filled with dairy cattle, and farmhouses shaded by tall cottonwood and Dutch elm. I take a left on

Fir Road and drive past a large apple orchard that overlooks Taylor Flats. At the bottom of the hill, where the dirt road forks, we follow the river upstream on a primitive one-track, loose cobble road that skirts the edge of a sheer rock wall. "Hold on tight," I say to Ken, weighing the risk of bending the right side-view mirror back versus rolling my truck into the yawning river below. I flashback to when I rode a lop-eared rental mule into Zion Canyon and saw nothing but empty space between me and my trusty steed when I made the mistake of peering over the edge of the trail. The word *vertigo* came to mind.

The last quarter mile of travel requires that we stop twice to scout safe passage where the road is washed out. One more leap of faith and we reach the end of the road. From the sign of things, few anglers have driven this far, although a collection of spent .22 and 30.06 casings indicates a popular location for target shooting.

I first visited this remote side-channel when I worked on an aquatic monitoring study of a nearby nuclear power plant in the 1970s. On a lark, we piloted a boat electroshocker along the shoreline and turned up several steelhead. I returned the next day with a box of spinners in my back pocket. This stretch of river, sometimes referred to as "Car Body Beach" because of abandoned vehicle wrecks, became a favorite place to fish for steelhead. When my field activities transitioned to more mundane desk duty, I flexed work time to arrive on the water at sunrise and fished until morning shadows disappeared.

Pound-for-pound, no freshwater fish fights harder than a steelhead. They swim faster and jump higher than other species of Pacific salmon. Some populations have the capacity to migrate over 2,000 miles to the ocean and back, spawn, survive all obstacles, and do it again. To many anglers, the sea-going version of rainbow trout, *Oncorhynchus mykiss*, is revered. There's no greater challenge than to take them on a fly.

Ken and I rig up our Spey rods, tiptoe across a wood plank that spans a deep gully and hike a narrow trail littered with coyote scat full of grape seeds from a nearby vineyard. Large alder, willow, and a thick band of reed canary grass cover a narrow cobble shoreline devoid of human traffic. "I like this spot," Ken says, staking out a shallow riffle that looks fishy. Thinking I got the short end of the deal, I set up a comfortable distance upstream where current breaks along a shoreline point. That's when I notice I missed a rod guide due to poor coordination or bad eyesight. Either way, I waste valuable fishing time re-stringing my rod.

Searching through an over-stuffed box of steelhead flies, I select a Dr. Bill. There's something to be gained by staying faithful to your first love. I tie it on 10-pound test tippet and scan the water's surface for eddies and roils – places where steelhead might take refuge. Fifty yards upstream of my position, the rusted body of an abandoned vehicle juts out from the shoreline to slow the current. A second wreck is plastered to the hill slope near where I parked my truck. I hope to *not* add to the collection, that I can maneuver my truck back to the main road safely.

The extra length of my 13-foot, 6-inch Loomis two-hander allows me to cast farther and with less effort than my 9-foot Cortland one-hander, which is an advantage on the Columbia River when wind is in your face. Although I have held a fly rod in my hand since I was 10, I am a novice in the art of Spey casting. My casting skill can be likened to how I cross-country ski on hard-packed snow. It ain't pretty but I get the job done.

I let water swirl around my ankles and settle into a steady rhythm of casting and retrieving, lengthening casts as I become more comfortable. The slightest change in tension gets your attention when you swing a fly – whether from the subtle grab of a fish or loose debris in the current – because there's nothing between you and the hook on the end of your line. I grip my rod lightly and seek to become one with the river. A voice in my head reminds, *one step, three casts.* Unfortunately, I rarely place three good casts in a row. Other places look good enough to merit a dozen or more casts. Regardless, I shuffle my feet, move downstream, and reposition.

Speculating how my fly might look to a steelhead fills in empty moments. *Will its size, shape, or the sparkle of sunbeams trapped in the dubbing trigger a steelhead's feeding instinct? Although purple is purported to be more visible at depth than other color spectrums, I'm not aware of any aquatic prey that come in that color. Maybe a steelhead will be attracted by my fly's undulating motion. Or maybe food has nothing to do with it and they want to kick its ass.*

Puffy clouds stack up on the eastern horizon to crowd out the morning sun and a light breeze ruffles the water's surface. Halfway down the run, I feel a sharp tug, my line tightens, and the water surface explodes. The drag on my reel sings the tune of a deep-bodied steelhead taking out line fast. Things quickly get out of control when it reverses direction and makes a long arcing run toward the shoreline. Operating in panic mode now, I back up to retrieve slack line, pirouette on my good leg, and almost go down. Luckily, I recover in time to find that it is still on.

Another long run towards midstream is followed by a second spectacular leap. I gain line as the steelhead holds position on the inside of the current seam, back to where it all began. It's stage two of the battle now and I'm feeling confident enough to try and lead the chrome bright fish to shallow water. Still with fight, it resists my intention. When I lean forward and strain to see an adipose fin, the steelhead turns its head from side-to-side, shakes the source of its torment loose, and swims free.

It was as if the prettiest girl on the dance floor had picked me to walk her home, only to toss her soft curls at me and say good-bye before we reached the front porch steps. "So much for a photo op," I say to Ken, who had put his rod down and wandered up the bank to watch the action.

"That's too bad," he replies. "What fly were you using?"

Three hours, 100 steps, and more than 300 casts later, we break our rods down and hike back to my truck. There's an old adage that states, "It's better to have loved and lost than never to have loved at all." The same notion rings true when it comes to chasing the elusive steelhead.

BURY ME with my fly rod

Went Fishing, But Did Not Fish

SOME BEST-LAID PLANS don't work out like you imagine. Consider the bitter-cold winter day when Ken and I went fishing but didn't fish. We didn't sneak off to a neighborhood bar to discuss politics or a warm coffee shop to hide behind a best-selling novel. We didn't frequent a strip-joint. The possibility entered our minds but the nearest one is 40 miles away and doesn't open until 4 p.m. We didn't get in a car wreck or experience a medical emergency. Failure to slip on our insulated stocking foot waders and rig up fly rods had nothing to do with lack of dedication. Our intentions were good. It's just that conditions did not merit making a single cast.

Competition for a good stretch of water did not exist on the day we did not fish because wind howled from the north at a steady

30 miles per hour, air temperature hovered around freezing, and moody skies hinted of sleet. Admittedly, the morning started off badly when I left my reel at home, an indiscretion that surfaced when I loaded my gear in Ken's truck at the gas station where we always meet. "A place of mutual inconvenience," I call it. Nobody comes out ahead on the commute. In the case of forgotten fishing equipment, we both come out behind.

Ken was kind enough to drive back to my house to retrieve the reel, after which we headed to the Hanford Reach to swing flies at complacent steelhead. An hour lost on a day when the odds of success are low is not always a crime.

Because neither of us felt like braving the elements, we ate an early lunch and watched whitecaps crash the shore from the comfort of Ken's truck. That's when Ken reached back in time with a story about a camping trip with two buddies in college. Beer drinking was involved – most likely in excess of the daily requirement. As Ken recalled, someone said, "Let's see who can pee the highest on this tree."

Ken did not share who won, so I assumed he came in either second or third, but the concept peaked my interest. "I don't think there is a training manual for that activity." I said.

"It's not likely training is required," Ken replied

Speaking of throwback behavior, I fired up a bowl of recent-legalized "whacky tobacky." Two hits later, I was on a roll. (The stuff is a lot stronger than when I was in college.) "Peeing for distance is like seeing who can spit a cherry seed the farthest in that trajectory and imparted pressure influence the distance of travel." I said. "My guess is peeing distance is mostly about the amount of fluid in your bladder. That, and how strong your smooth muscles are, which means age is also a factor."

To which Ken replied, "He with the most pressure pees the

highest."

"Straddle the base of the tree and let it fly."

This exchange of bathroom humor reminds of a story by author Tom Robbins, who described how he and fellow classmates lined up in the woods during school recess to see who could pee the farthest. Some boys went so far as to ask interested female observers to tap their penis for good luck. I suspect such encouragement increased their peeing distance.

After the topic of peeing dried up, I proposed to Ken that we find a stretch of protected shoreline. Someplace where we might cast unencumbered by the harsh elements. Where hard hats and goggles were not required as protection against random head slaps from errant-cast flies. A short drive upriver found us opposite the old Hanford townsite where we once again elected to remain in the comfort of the truck and watch whitecaps crash against exposed cobble.

"It's impossible to cast with a strong wind in your face," I said. "And if that ain't enough, the water level is too low for steelhead to hold along this shoreline. How about we hike over to the river and speculate where to cast on a nice day when flows are acceptable?"

We tightened our ball caps a notch and got out of the truck. On the way to the river, I spotted a small bird clinging to the top of a big sage, pointing like a weather vane into the relentless wind. "What kind of bird is that?" I asked Ken.

"It's a horned lark," he replied.

"Hmmm, I guess I haven't seen one for awhile," I said. "Either that, or I confuse them with meadowlarks."

Like the handsome poker player, Bart Maverick, once said, "Some things you forget, if you notice them at all."

Hiking across a wide bench that led to the river above the flood plain, I remarked to Ken that he looked down while he walked. "I always watch for snakes," he replied. 'It comes from working in rattlesnake country most of my life."

In contrast, I rarely look at my feet. I just go – more focused on the endpoint than how I get there. It's my world through the windshield view. Not looking down can lead to stepping on dog doo though, something which happens to me more often than I care to admit. The irony is that Ken stepped in a burrowing animal hole while he soaked up details of the ground, tripped, and almost fell down.

Ken's keen observational skills returned to form once we reached the river. As an example, he pointed out impressions made by tumbleweeds where wind had whisked them across the wetted edge of river cobble. I focused my attention on the river, speculating where steelhead might reside when rocks were covered with water. Big picture things that relate to fishing should not get confused with minutia.

On the hike back to the truck, Ken stopped to scan a faraway flock of ducks and geese. "Want to see?" he asked, offering his binoculars.

"No," I replied. "I know what Canada geese look like and the ducks are too far away for me to identify. I'm content to watch them fly."

Libation seemed appropriate after our brief sojourn, so we opened our coolers. "Want one of my beers?" Ken said. (He always brings an extra for me.)

"Thanks, but I'll stick with what I brought," I answered.

There are several reasons for your choice of beer: you like the flavor, you appreciate the fact it's on sale, it doesn't upset your G.I. tract, or maybe a certain lager or ale makes you more regular. You might drink a particular brand because your friends drink it and you want to fit in. Television ads that show sexy people laughing and having fun might cause you to try it. Some people settle for mixed variety packs with attractive labels from Costco. It's also possible that a bottle feels good in your hand. Tall "Buds" and Corona "long necks" do that for me.

Ken is a hophead. In beer-drinker language, this means he favors IPAs over other varieties of brew. I prefer red ales, although a simple lager, such as a PBR ("selected as America's finest in 1893"), fits the bill when I am relaxing in my favorite Adirondack chair. Of course, drinking beer leads to eating snacks, so Ken and I killed off a 7-ounce bag of Tim's Cascade Style potato chips. I call the act of eating a bag of Tim's chips in a single setting "having a Tim's fit." Another term would be "getting the munchies."

If I had only one food group to take into Heaven, it might be potato chips. The bottom of bag, where the crunchy dime-size bits soak up salt and grease, contains the "hashish" of potato chips. Mainlining a handful of these delectable crumbs and shoving them in your mouth without consideration for spillage is like going for the gold.

Ken and I weren't expected home until dinner, so I proposed that we hunt for agates. Low water exposes tiny geologic treasures along the Columbia River, similar to how receding ocean tides reveal colorful glass balls and dead starfish on coastal beaches. "Agate hunting hones your habitat association skills," I said to Ken, hoping to appeal to the naturalist side of his brain.

Ken was silent. It wasn't clear if he agreed with my suggestion or if he didn't feel like arguing. Nonetheless, without an idea of his own to share, we headed for Taylor Flats.

I've wandered the shorelines of the Hanford Reach for over five decades. Nowadays, I'll often take a break from a hard day of fishing to look for agates. Agates aren't worth much, except to hold up to the light and argue about their color or degree of translucence. Finding one, however, makes you feel better about not catching fish.

I often joke about setting up a display table on a touristy, ocean-side parking lot to sell bolo ties that showcase my agate collection. Gold-colored agates are my favorite, but white ones are okay, especially if they are large or have an intricate pattern. I don't secure the first agate that I find in my pants pocket until a second or a third one is found. The idea is one agate in hand begets another.

After harvesting half a dozen small agates, Ken and I hiked up a bunchgrass-covered slope to soak in a panoramic view of the river. In the distance were gravel bar islands, chalk-white vertical bluffs, sage-dotted flats, giant sand dunes, and concrete monoliths that remind of the Atomic Age. These things are rarely noticed when you are fishing.

The short drive back to the gas station and my truck was capped off with a spirited discussion about the relative merits of Milky Ways versus Snickers and the optimum mass, that is the Halloween version, regular, or giant size, required to satisfy your sweet tooth.

"I prefer regular-size Snickers," Ken started off. "I like the peanuts."

"Ever had Almond Snickers?" I asked.

"Those are Mars bars," Ken replied.

"No. They quit making Mars bars over ten years ago. Mars bars were topped with two almonds and covered with chocolate. Almond Snickers are similar to regular Snickers except they contain bits of almond instead of peanuts. "

"I'll have to try one sometime," he said.

These are a few things that occurred on a cold and windy day in January when Ken and I went fishing for steelhead but did not fish. I've never been known to push religion on anyone, but sometimes you have to make the best of what the good Lord serves and go with it.

My Zen Moment

A GUTTED, HEADLESS FALL Chinook salmon hangs by its tail from a nylon rope that an angler tied to the passenger-side mirror of his vintage Winnebago. The smell of decaying algae mixes with that of rotting fish. Half a dozen plunkers recline in lawn chairs at the mouth of Hatchery Creek, ignoring a spin fisherman who casts a golf ball-size chunk of roe over the top of them. Two middle-aged men, one attired in brown coveralls, the other wearing shorts and a sleeveless camo shirt, kneel at the water's edge filleting their catch. A steady hum from motor craft serenade dark-bodied salmon that roll and jump as if to show they can. Ring-bill gulls strut about like barnyard chickens, scrapping for discarded fish guts and old bait. The only thing missing from the bawdy scene is a shifty-eye guy hawking cheap watches.

I get out of my truck near where Art rests on a small canvas stool and step over a dead sucker baking in the October sun. Art, a recent convert to Spey casting, shares that he has been swinging his favorite steelhead pattern downstream of the cluster of salmon anglers since daylight. "I'm worn out," he says, before nodding to indicate where our friend, Dick, stands ankle-deep in the river. "Just look at him. He's effortless."

"A Zen master with the fly rod," I reply.

Dick is not just a man standing in the shallows. His actions are as fluid as the current that flows around his ankles. He is an extension of the river as manifested by the seamless connection between his fly rod, line, and fly. Each cast is an affirmation of faith.

These things I sense largely as a result of familial osmosis, starting when my wife joined a neighborhood Sangha and, later, when my son became a certified yoga instructor. The only time I embraced ancient Eastern philosophy was in college, when ganja-induced discussion supported by the melody of Ravi Shankar's sitar led that direction. Although a few years back, I started my daily exercise regimen captivated by a television contortionist who demonstrated impossible yoga positions to a group of lithe young women garbed in black tights, loose-fitting T-shirts, and no apparent undergarments. After that inspiring cable offering was replaced by a string of reality home repair shows, I relied on memory to perform poses such as the Mountain, Warrior, and Down Dog. Lately, I'm more inclined to start my day off with stretches and deep-breathing exercises that stimulate the deep core. Either that or I lie on the dining room floor, watch cloud formations sail by the window, wait for coffee to perk, and ignore that my 24-year-old cockatiel, Spike, is making frantic love to his ever-faithful, tiny silver bell.

It had been a year since my last two-handed casting lesson from Dick on the lower Deschutes River and I was in dire need of a tune up. Dick drove his motor home to the Hanford Reach of the Columbia River to fish for steelhead each fall. By his own admission, he had been Spey casting for over two decades. In contrast, I had a no more than a leap year of casual practice under my belt.

Not long after I arrive on the scene, fellow angler Gary wanders over to get in on our tête-à-tête. Gary is a passionate fly fisher with simple tastes. He doesn't carry a fly box filled with fifty different patterns and he doesn't have an $800 fly rod. What he does have is a mental map of every feature of the shoreline and a pleasant orneriness that allows him to carry on a conversation with anyone willing to match wits.

Taking advantage of a lull in action, a young fish checker approached our affable group with the standard two questions: "Catch anything?" and "How long have you been fishing?"

"Nothing here. Give me two hours at it," Gary replies, before asking, "What's that hammer for? Going to hit a fish over the head with it? Or maybe us, if we don't cooperate?"

Not to be dissuaded by his friendly banter, she explains her handheld tool is an instrument for "checking metal tags."

Gary warms to the task. "See that guy down there?" he says, gesturing to Dick, who works a shallow run upstream of the irrigation return canal like it was the only game in town. "You better check him. Rumor is he caught a ten-pound wild steelhead this morning and hid it in the brush."

"Is he a friend of yours?" she asks.

"Not really," I reply. "That's why he's down there all by himself."

To which Gary adds, "He doesn't have any friends."

Ten minutes go by before Dick plods over to join in on our merriment. "How'd it go with the fish checker?" Art asks.

"She told me what you guys said about me," Dick replies.

After sharing a good laugh at Dick's expense, conversation diverted to his latest Spey rod.

"What did you pay for that one?" Gary asks.

"It cost twelve-hundred, but I got it for thirty percent off," Dick replies.

After acknowledging Dick's classy Simms waders, Gary puffs up his chest and points to his aged Hodgeman hip boots. "I bought these for fifty-nine bucks."

I take notice of his frugality before shining attention back to Dick. "What happened to your zippered waders?"

"They weren't worth the extra two hundred dollars," he replied, which led to a string of pee stories.

"It's tough to get your member out when it's cold and windy."

"I'd like to know why you have to pee five minutes after getting into a float tube even though you just voided your bladder."

"I think it's the extra pressure of being surrounded by water."

"Maybe you imbibe water. Like a germinating seed."

By now, an hour and a half of a balmy Indian summer afternoon had passed without me catching a fish or solving a single problem of the world. I flush my brain of extraneous thought and finish stringing up my Loomis two-hander. Armed with a killer fly bummed from Dick's overflowing box of a dozen proven patterns, I cross Hatchery Creek and head upstream in search of a patch of boulders distant from the crowd of rabid salmon anglers. A well-trodden trail skirts a shoreline crowded with cattail and willow. Several shallow ditches, constructed by beavers as escape routes during low river flow, requires your attention, as does wet cobble greasy with a skin of decomposed algae. When Dick and I approach a stretch of water known as Split Rock, I scan the surface for disruption in flow; features that lead me to places where a steelhead might rest.

I slip into the river. The Zen master takes position a safe distance away and provides several pointers to get me started, after which I thrash the water with a competing breeze in my face. "Do you swing your fly or do you allow it to dead drift?" I ask as a diversionary tactic following one particularly bad cast.

"I swing my fly," Dick replies.

My Intruder swings across the gentle current while I imagine how it looks to a steelhead with opinion. More important, I settle into a comfortable technique that proves effective up to four casts in a row. Still, I detect quiet scrutiny from Dick. "Keep moving," he directs, when I pause too long at a promising section of broken water.

Despite a menacing stand of coyote willow that lurks within range of my back cast, I get better. Technique-wise, it is mostly a matter of staying off my toes, keeping my D-loop close, and not going with too much top hand. *Or so it seems.* I park my pride and shorten casting distance, a tactic that results in more precise offerings. Lacking a clear target, however, casting into a river a half-mile wide occasionally put me in the "flock shoot" mode, leading to errant casts. "That's one good thing about barbless hooks," Dick remarks when I hook my shirt collar on one particularly sloppy retrieve. "They are easier to remove from your ear than the barbed version."

Zen Buddhism teaches that the moon serves as a metaphor for an experience of enlightenment, but that any attempt to articulate a philosophy or true meaning of faith is merely "a finger pointing at the moon." Considering the holistic nature of these teachings, it follows there should be no confounding of the moon with a finger. On this balmy autumn afternoon, I wonder if the moon in my fly fishing universe is a steelhead and my Spey rod the finger.

Putting aspiration toward achieving discovery in wisdom aside, I sense the river is my inseparable companion, one where I strive to operate in the "here and now." Always a daydreamer, however, my quandary is staying on task. I visualize how my fly merges with water particles. I ponder cumulus clouds skating across the sky. I inventory scrape marks made by suckers on algae-covered rock. The flat light of afternoon sun projecting off sage-dotted hills demands attention, as do the twitter of California quail and the musty odor of wet cobble.

According to Buddha, "The mind is everything. What you think, you become." Reflecting on these words, I step outside the scattered thoughts in my head and let my mind join with the river. Time stands still when my fly disappears into a current seam downstream of where water crests over a waist-high boulder and I am rewarded with a two-part take. An initial line-straightening grab, followed by a sharp tug, brings me out of my reverie. Unfortunately, when I raise my rod tip to set the hook, the steelhead is off.

"I had a grab!" I yell.

"I saw it," the Zen master replies. Then, as if reciting a parable from the Fly Fisher Bible, he explains, "You need to lower your rod tip if the take occurs directly below you. Give the steelhead a chance to eat the fly before you set the hook. Otherwise, you'll pull it out of their mouth."

"I got excited," is the best I can come up with. Although I placed my fly in front of a cooperative steelhead – whether due to buck fever or incompetence – I missed my chance. Yet a certain sense of trueness transcended at the instant the steelhead grabbed the fly and my line tightened. It was as if a loop closed, providing a feeling that was both distinct and not distinct. However fleeting the moment, it made me mindful of place. I had become immersed in totality.

It was my Zen moment.

Summer steelhead that pass through or overwinter the Hanford
Reach of the Columbia River can be taken swinging a fly.

Secret Family Recipes, Part Deux

SMOKED STEELHEAD

Filet a medium-sized hatchery steelhead and cut the filets into "swatches" 3 to 4 inches in diameter. Rinse off excess slime and wipe the skin dry with a paper towel. Put a single layer of meat, skin side down, in the bottom of a large plastic container with a locking lid. Coat the meat thoroughly with a 4:1 brown sugar to salt mixture. Add additional layers of meat and repeat adding dry brine. Seal the container and place in the refrigerator overnight. While your morning coffee perks, wipe excess brine and slime from each swatch, lay the meat on paper towels, and allow it to reach room temperature. Fire up your smoker and place the brined meat on racks skin side down. Occasionally switch racks to ensure even cooking. Smoking takes from 4 to 12 hours depending on the age of your smoker and outside air temperature. Don't try to finish smoked fish off in the microwave or oven. I did that once and caught the wrath of wife Nancy because our house smelled like smoked fish for a week.

PBJ SANDWICH

There's nothing like a peanut butter and jam sandwich for a high-energy snack, whether eaten with your fly line dangling in the water (can lead to a strike) or while you sit on a fat log (can lead to bites from a carpenter ant). PBJs are virtually indestructible. You can drop them on the ground, leave them on the front seat of your truck, and shove them in a pocket of a gear vest. The outcome may not be pretty, but your sandwich will maintain its integrity. Half a PBJ can be ingested in less time than it takes to strip in 50 feet of backing. A whole PBJ provides the calories to walk two miles and tastes far better than a Clif Bar. I prefer to marry my Skippy peanut butter with raspberry jam. Apricot jam works equally well, as does strawberry. My fishing buddy, Ken, opts for jelly because he doesn't like to pick seeds from his teeth. For me, the extra flavor and texture of jam makes seed management trivial. A PBJ on white bread takes you back to your childhood, while one made with 12-grain makes you feel healthy. The choices are endless.

Dusty Dauble and Rick Huizinga prepare a rental raft for a float from Trout Creek to Maupin.

PART THREE. EPIC ANGLING TALES

THIS IS JUST A STORY OF SOME RODS AND THE PLACES
THEY TAKE YOU TO

-NEGLEY FARSON

BURY ME with my fly rod

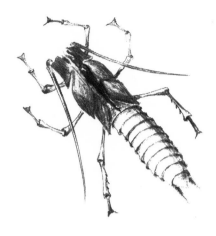

Big Dog and Salmon Flies

My brother, Dusty, his long-time pal, Rick, and I beached our overloaded rubber raft near milepost 76 to take advantage of the only privy within four miles. It was early June and the last morning of a four-day float trip on the Deschutes River. I was bed sore, scratched and sunburned. The poison oak on my left arm and neck had festered into something resembling leprosy and I wondered where on my body it would show up next. Gazing across the river from the top step of the privy, I spotted the dark form of a long-legged canine loping through a stand of juniper. I couldn't help but blurt, "Look. It's a wolf!"

As soon as the words flew out of my mouth, I felt stupid. It couldn't possibly be a timber wolf. Wolves resided in the northern Cascades and the wilds of central Idaho, not on the Warm Springs Indian Reservation in central Oregon. *But what breed of hundred-pound dog maneuvers across the face of a steep rock bluff with the deft motion of an Olympic slalom skier and disappears into a small cave?*

I was a relative newcomer to the Deschutes River, having spent a single day casting for "redsides" near Warm Springs a few years back. In contrast, Dusty and Rick made annual pilgrimages to what is arguably the most iconic trout stream in the Pacific Northwest. I was eager to test my skills though, having never seriously tossed flies for trout in moving water outside of nearby Crooked River and a cadre of Blue Mountain streams. Floating the Deschutes also presented opportunity for an extended camping trip, one dedicated entirely to fishing.

Our float trip coincided with the annual salmon fly hatch. Every year, around the end of May, these impressive insects emerge from the depths of the river, crawl onto rocks and shoreline vegetation, and transform into winged adults. The Deschutes River is home to several species of stoneflies that range from ½ inch to 3 inches long. Mixed in with a giant red-body version are "little sallies" and medium-sized golden stones. Variability in size and color produce dozens of fly patterns for anglers hoping to match the hatch.

During all the commotion, the resident trout population abandons their senses. It's the season when any fly casting novice can catch a world-class rainbow. At least that's what local fly shops try to make you think. Angling websites had exploded with positive press for over a month. "The trout are now entirely keyed in on the stones throughout the Maupin area and to the locked gate and above." "A bonanza of stonefly activity." "The trout are ready for them."

Other descriptors, like intense, mega, awesome, mind-blowing, and unforgettable, peppered daily blogs designed to entice anglers to fill their fly box with a few dozen extra hand-tied dries. But this float trip was not all about tossing big hairy patterns. Caddisflies, mayflies, and midgeflies also entice Deschutes River trout. The setting was prime for what all fly-fishing aficionados dream about when they aren't eating Canadian bacon and Eggs Benedict served by white-coated waiters at a $2,000 per day lodge in Chile.

The Deschutes River was an angler's Mecca by all accounts. However, learning how to catch trout there required that I step well outside my comfort zone.

DAY ONE

I left home in the Tri-Cities before first light with a sack of day-old donuts and a thermos of coffee riding shotgun beside me. A steady diet of guitar licks delivered by Jimi Hendrix, the Jerry Garcia Band, and the Mermen kept me alert. Driving music. I passed through a series of ominous storm fronts on the freeway between Umatilla and Biggs, including one with the appearance of a tornado. Rain pelted the windshield when I arrived in Maupin to transfer gear into the back of Rick's vintage GMC truck for the hour-long commute to Trout Creek.

I tried to remain upbeat. Fishing trips were not meant to be spent hiding from rain. I was also apprehensive about white water rafting, having never floated dangerous rapids. Equally important, I wondered if I would be asked to row. Finally, I was concerned about not knowing what we were going to eat and when we would eat it. Admittedly, much of my angst stemmed from lack of information about the trip. I'd never been good about trusting the unknown, despite being immersed in organized religion for much of my life.

I recalled an early conversation with Dusty, when I pressed

for detail about meals. "Breakfast is covered, but why don't you bring eight pieces of KFC for the first night." He said. "Rick will cook pork steaks on the second night and I'll bring something for the third."

"Can't we eat fresh fish one night?" I replied. "The Deschutes has a two-trout limit."

"Rick is strict about catch and release. Maybe you could bring a piece of salmon."

"I'm not bringing frozen salmon when I could eat fresh trout."

It could have gone on like that all night, except I blurted, "What other behaviors do you old guys have that I need to know about before I sign up for the trip?"

Rather than answer straightforward, Dusty rebuked, as only an older brother can do. "That's ridiculous," he said. "You're as old as we are."

When I shared the exchange with my friend Geoff, he cautioned me not to go. "I'm telling you right now," he said. "It's not going to work out."

I pondered Geoff's sage advice at Trout Creek, where we competed for shoreline space with a steady stream of cold and miserable rafters landing from upstream launch sites. Our camping gear was spread out over a 50-square-yard patch of wet orchard grass: coolers, folding chairs, sleeping bags, pads, tent, pillows, portable toilet, fishing rods, beer, pop, bottled water, ice, snacks, and more snacks. You can never have too many snacks. Everything had to be stowed in a dry bag and secured to the 14-foot rental raft before we could push off. I wanted to assist, but didn't know enough about the process to insert myself, so I stood by while Rick methodically packed our goods and equipment.

My sense of wellbeing nosedived when Dusty and Rick raised

their eyebrows at my half-rack of PBR. "What's that?" Dusty said in a tone that implied middle-America's finest lager did not merit equal space in the ice chest with their bottled microbrew.

"It's boat beer," I replied. "Cans take up less space in the garbage sack than bottles if you crush the empties."

Dusty's lips did not move, but his eyes said, "I'd better not see your hands around a bottle of my Heineken."

When I looked to Rick for moral support, he ignored me, all the while sipping on a Black Butte Porter. Meanwhile, a seasonal park ranger busted Dusty for flicking a cigarette butt on the ground next to a large sign that reminded smoking was banned on the stream bank. *What is there about my brother that results in a reprimand from an authority figure nearly every time we go fishing?* I thought.

More disconcerting was a notice pasted to the lower part of the "No Smoking" sign: "Open camp fires are not permitted starting June 1." I didn't expect a fire ban. It hardly seemed warranted given the recent rainstorm. A camping trip without a fire is like getting a massage with your clothes on.

Meanwhile, the two-man shuttle crew was antsy to get back to Maupin before lunch. Pacing nervously between our raft and Rick's truck, they dropped remarks like: "You've got a lot of stuff" and "Need help loading your gear?"

Their frenetic presence merely added to Rick's stress, but he ignored them while Dusty and I chatted with other anglers. Although Rick could be characterized as "deliberate," he was the kind of guy you want on your team. He had his list and he checked it twice. If a dry bag looked out of balance, he swapped it out for another. If a rope was loose, he retraced its steps to the proper carabineer and cinched it down securely. *All good things take time*, I reminded myself.

Two hours later, gear finally strapped down to Rick's satisfaction, we shoved off. Rain had lessened and a light breeze stirred the water's surface. Scattered sunrays poked through ominous storm clouds clinging to ridge tops. An occasional trout rose along the shoreline, but the mythical salmon fly hatch appeared sparse.

Boning up on a few salient facts about the Deschutes River before the trip, I learned that flows in the 33-mile long stretch of river we planned to float were dependent on spring-fed tributaries and water storage practices of dams located further upriver. Diving deeper into regional history, I found that Lewis and Clark referred to the Deschutes by its Indian name, "Towornehiooks," and that early French trappers called the river, "le Riviere des Chutes," or "The River of the Falls." *But where were the rapids?* I wondered. The initial stretch of river downstream of Trout Creek offered only an occasional riffle to challenge our rafting skills. Dusty and I hung our feet over the side and amused ourselves down-rating shoreline anglers who casted weighted nymphs below strike indicators. Rick chimed in, "They're just bobber fishing. That ain't right!"

When I inquired about fly patterns, Rick made it clear that we were to fish dry flies or nothing. *So much for the bottom-bumping half of my fly box*, I thought. Three beers apiece, nine miles and two hours later, we arrived at Whiskey Dick, milepost 78. Rick nosed the raft onto a small sandy beach halfway down a designated camping area. On the Reservation side of the river, two anglers cast spinners next to a bedrock boulder the size a VW bug. Two hundred yards to the east was a railroad track that skirted a low hill covered with big sage, gray rabbitbrush, and the occasional juniper and ponderosa pine.

No sooner did we set up camp than Dusty crawled into the

tent to nap. Rick grabbed his fly rod and headed upstream, so I grabbed mine and hiked a respectable distance downstream. Starting with a Red Stone, I fished pocket water, deep runs, side channels, and swirl pools. I then switched to a series of Stimulators, No. 6 through No. 10, and repeated the drill. When that tactic failed to produce a take, I tied on patterns that had produced for me in home waters. The primary outcome of the frantic pattern-swapping exercise was a shorter tippet. It seemed the famous Deschutes River trout population was not as active as tackle shop hype would lead you to believe.

Frustrated, I tied on a beadhead nymph of unknown vintage and let it drift deep like a guided angler I saw earlier in the day. This ploy led to me hooking a 7-inch trout that waved goodbye on the first jump. Admittedly, it was difficult to concentrate on technique while looking over my shoulder to make sure Rick didn't catch me violating the sacred brotherhood of the dry fly.

The thing of it was, I knew about trout behavior in Blue Mountain streams. I didn't have to wait for a rise to know where they lived. My instincts had been honed from years of experience. Moreover, Blue Mountain trout readily rose to the fly in the middle of the day. But Deschutes trout were different. Whether because of poor technique or lack of knowledge, I could not bring a single trout to the fly.

Three hours of casting with nothing to show for my efforts was more than I could endure, so I walked back to camp, zigzagging through waist-high sagebrush. The afternoon had warmed to where I thought of shedding my chest waders, but their protection from poison oak and rattlesnakes was worth the discomfort. Back in camp, Dusty and Rick sat side by side in canvas chairs with a book in their lap. "Any luck?" I asked, hoping to learn the secret of how to catch a Deschutes redside.

Dusty casually replied, "I haven't been out yet. Thought I would give it a try after dinner."

Rick set aside his well-worn copy of *Confessions of a Corporate Hitman* to report that two different trout rose to his fly. He returned to his reading while I extracted myself from my waders, found a place in the sun, and napped. To say the least, their lack of interest was disconcerting.

As planned, dinner was KFC from the box. The main culinary challenge involved dividing the eight-piece meal three ways, but we managed to do so without conflict. Congealed grease aside, the chicken tasted like home cooking when washed down with personal brand of beer. We tossed chicken bones into the river while an upriver breeze jostled the tent and nighthawks chased bugs overhead with the skill of F-15 fighter pilots.

Earlier that afternoon, another raft landed a short distance downstream and tethered to the shoreline. The oarsman set up a large sleeping tent with cots and a dining tent that he populated with assorted tables and chairs. While we ate cold KFC, a gray-bearded guide and two anglers arrived in a drift boat. It was a guided trip with all the trimmings. The four of them sipped white wine in a lantern-lit tent while we nursed our assigned brand of beer, swatted mosquitoes, discussed advanced rod prop design, and argued whether it was more ecologically responsible to pee in the river or on the ground.

This discourse took place while we reclined in $6.99 canvas chairs with built-in mesh drink holders. Rick offered a guess at what the couple's trip cost. "I saw a three-day guided trip advertised for $2,900 a person," he said.

I did the math. "Let's say $400 a day for the guide and support raft, plus another $200 for camping amenities, plus food, plus what else? It still doesn't add up," I said, appreciative of our

$50 a day do-it-yourself scenario. Still, I imagined a fold-up canvas cot would work wonders for my sore back.

Dusty finally took a turn at casting when fingers of shadows began to stretch across the river. As if by script, he hooked two large trout, while I wondered what he knew that I didn't. "He always has good luck here," Rick explained. "That's why we chose this site for the first night."

Meanwhile, I thrashed the water with a series of tried and true patterns that failed to generate a single hookset. "Tomorrow will be better," Rick promised. "The stones should be more active once it warms up. Don't be chagrined. The best fishing is yet to come."

Chagrined was an accurate description of my feelings at the time, although it's not a word I use in conversation on a regular basis.

Day Two

I turned over in my vintage mummy bag three times during the night, which is as good as it gets when you sleep on the ground. Coyotes serenaded a series of yelps, barks, yodels, and howls while the valley remained cloaked in shade. I crawled out of the tent, leaving Dusty snoring a low resonance suggestive of a mind at ease. Rick dozed quietly next to the fire pit after opting to spend a cosmic night under a cascade of stars. The well-worn trail to the outhouse was active from a large group of anglers who camped in an alder grove farther upstream.

There's a story about these privies. The U.S. Bureau of Land Management has preference for placing them on high elevation cobble and boulder bars that were deposited by Holocene-period floodwaters approximately 4,400 years ago. These past flow events have since been named "outhouse floods." Having ready access to a covered one-holer is a huge upgrade from scraping a hole in the ground or toting waste from place-to-place in a "honey bucket."

I felt displaced. I wasn't excited about fishing, given my lack of success from the day before, and I didn't feel bold enough about my place in the camp hierarchy to start breakfast, so I sat in my designated canvas chair while bank swallows swooped over the river. The flute-like call of a meadowlark floated from upland sage. Redwing blackbirds chortled from shoreline reeds. An acrid smell of juniper filled the air. It was hard to imagine being anywhere else.

I remained cautious about camp duties when my companions woke up, figuring I'd watch and learn before jumping into the mix. As things turned out, breakfast wasn't all that complicated. The first order of business was to boil water for a French press after which Dusty fried up link sausage and scrambled eggs amended with Gruyere cheese and a sprinkle of fresh sage. Plates and utensils were brought out, food was consumed, and dishes were washed. That's how camping is supposed to work. The only challenge is who does what and when. My mood improved. I felt like a sinner brought back into the fold – a believer in trout and the Deschutes River.

Meanwhile, a steady line-up of rafts floated by camp as if part of a holiday parade. Only when a drift boat with cots stacked four-high passed did we make a move. This time I helped Rick load the raft, receptive about when to assist and when to let him direct. Dusty stood nearby and entertained with a story about Whitehorse, the famous two-mile long Class IV rapid we would soon encounter. He became uncharacteristically animated when he described getting dumped on what he called "Oh Shit" Rock. "I stayed with the raft for awhile, but it kept pushing me down. I was stuck under it," he said. "Finally, everyone yelled at me to go to shore so I let go and swam for it."

Rick chimed in. "We had gear hanging from trees and spread on rocks for several yards along the shoreline. Jim lost his fly rod when the raft turned over, so we had to share fishing time for the rest of the trip. That's also when Dusty lost your Grandpa's split bamboo rod."

A light bulb went off inside my head. So that's why Dusty mentioned that he didn't row anymore. The harrowing experience scared the holy heck out of him and led to the loss of a prized family heirloom. The greater issue was whether I had the skill to maneuver dangerous rapids if I had to substitute for Rick on the oars.

The river gave no hint of what was to come as we floated lazily on the mile-long drift to upper Whitehorse Rapids. On reaching the overlook, Rick nosed our raft onto a steep mud bank lined with poison oak. We clambered up a well-worn trail, hiked down the railroad tracks, squatted above the river, and peered through overhanging alder to scout a safe route. "See that slot?" Rick asked, pointing to a diffuse feature in a half-mile long boil of white water studded with huge boulders. "We need to hit it there and row hard towards the right bank. Then I'll cross back over to the left before we get to House Rock."

I nodded agreement without having a clue how Rick would make a clean shot through the tumultuous rapids. Although I prided myself in knowing how to read water for trout, deciphering a safe route through Whitehorse was information overload. The odds of coming out unscathed looked like a crapshoot. Maybe it was better I didn't fully grasp the implication of river rafting. The ability to let your mind go under time of pressure has its benefits.

Strapping on life jackets for the first time since leaving Trout Creek, we pushed off from shore. Dusty sobered, perhaps reflecting on his previous near-death experience. Rick was also quiet, but in a concentrative way. He pointed the bow of the raft toward the churning commotion and picked up pace on the oars. Dusty grabbed onto the bow rope and I gripped the side rail as we entered the slipstream that pulled us towards the head of the rapids. It was time for old-fashioned religion in the form of silent prayer. The nose of our raft rode the crest of the first curl, plunged into a boiling trough, and sent a sheet of cold water over my head. I was drenched, but didn't dare let go of my handhold to wipe my sunglasses clear.

"There's Oh Shit," Dusty yelled when we blew past a giant boulder with a million gallons of water per second spilling over it. Rick later told me the rock was a legend. Not because of its immense size, but because of its determining position in the rapids and a "pointy head" that snags rafters and drift boaters who misjudge their route. I imagined what it would feel like to hit the boulder at 30 miles per hour and pushed the thought out of my mind. Meanwhile our raft twisted sideways in the current, while Rick fought the oars to maintain a straightforward position. We bobbed and weaved past House Rock, just missing another big boulder hidden beneath the water's surface. I sensed the worst was over when Dusty (still with a tight grip on his security rope) leaned forward to compliment Rick's rowing.

"The run was easier than last year," Rick yelled above the roar of pounding water, working the raft toward the east bank where the current slowed. "Having higher flow helped. Usually, there are more rocks sticking out of the water."

Exhilarated from our successful run through what some boaters consider to be the most dangerous rapids in the river, we beached the raft and tied off to shore. It wasn't until Dusty and Rick discussed where to camp that I realized our float was done for the day. We scrutinized a wide flat spot between the shoreline and the railroad embankment, but rejected it – lack of shade. A nearby site, tucked between alder and juniper and known to some rafters as "Frenchy's," had a rustic wooden bench for storing cooking utensils, broken-off juniper branches for hanging fishing equipment, and ready access to a walking path along the railroad tracks. A decision was made. Gear was unloaded and we set up for the night.

Things got exciting in a hurry when Rick almost stepped on a three-foot long rattlesnake. Rather than chance having it slither into my sleeping bag, I fashioned a snare from a short length of clothesline cord and a juniper branch. "Don't worry, I've done this before," I said to Dusty and Rick, who watched with keen interest. I missed the rattler's head on the first pass but looped its 8-button tail on the second. Keeping wide-open fangs at arm's length, I deposited the writhing snake well down the railroad tracks.

The air over the river was filled with a welcoming party of giant Stones. Some were as long as my little finger, more resembling a bat than a swallow in flight. They flopped on the water's surface like winged acrobats, bounced off overhanging alder, crawled on exposed rocks, and hung from reed canary grass. Some individuals were paired up, their abdomens twisted together sidesaddle-like, in a death grip, as if sex is desperate.

Eager to wet a line, I walked down the railroad tracks to a promising stretch of water. With no obvious path to the river, I crouched and slid down the concrete-hard slope on the heels of my tennis shoes. Skidding like a novice snow-boarder on packed ice, I landed crosswise on a boulder, took a gash on the palm of my hand, and ripped the seat of my pants. However, no major injury resulted and I was quickly rewarded with a silver-sided 13-inch trout that struck an over-sized Yellow Stone that I had swiped from Rick's box of four dozen.

Thirty yards farther down the railroad embankment, a pair of big-shouldered trout rose to sip caddisflies. One fish worked heavy current next to a boulder. The other fish stationed at the inside of a current seam. They took turns feeding as if no care in the world while my adrenaline spiked. Neither fish responded to careful presentation though, apparently tuned to something other than what I had to offer. I left them and worked downstream to a huge hole that swirled across half the width of the river. Insect castings and other debris turned and twisted in the swirling current. Salmon flies bound up in surface tension were sucked down by never-ending rope vortices. Just out of reach of my longest cast, a large pod of trout ripped on caddisflies in a back eddy. More trout rose along a current line formed where a giant boulder deflected flow. Long dark shapes rose from depth and turned toward my Stimulator only to retreat.

I may be slow, but sooner or later things begin to add up. I tied on the smallest Elk Hair Caddis in my box and caught three trout in quick succession. It's funny how things work. I was no longer driven to catch a fish. Hooking and landing several trout had raised my self-esteem to where I could finally relax and enjoy the experience. I stripped to my briefs, jumped into the river, and rinsed off two days of sweat. While I sat on a flat boulder and dried off with my T-shirt, I spotted Dusty back at camp ransacking our ice chest in search of the bite-sized Almond Joys I had carefully hidden under the pasta salad. As he explained later, but not contritely, "I've got a sweet tooth."

Looking to explore, I headed downstream and found a shoreline exploding with the honey-sweet fragrance of mock orange in bloom. At the outside of the river bend, where flow spilled over a narrow basalt shelf, I took my best redside of the day, a large male that displayed brilliant crimson markings when it torpedoed from broken water to annihilate a No. 10 Orange Stone in a manner I had once expected on every cast.

Two days without obligation to anyone or anything put me in a tranquil state of mind. There was no burning desire to catch a self-imposed quota of fish. I stirred sandy soil that lay beneath a stately ponderosa pine, uncovering tiny beads of multi-colored pitch that glowed liked agates on an ocean beach. I admired clumps of bunchgrass tossing in the breeze, regaled in the slow glide of a red-tailed hawk riding a thermal, and pondered how caddisflies arranged their cases in the shallows. When tired of these diversions, I listened to the chirping of a nervous osprey in its nest on a power pole above the railroad tracks. Popcorn clouds floated over steep canyon walls. A gentle breeze rustled the leaves of streamside alders. Nature is a great playground if you are willing to dawdle.

"Do you feel more spiritual when you are here?" Rick asked me back at camp, stuffing his gray-flecked ponytail under a well-worn *Wild Trout* ball cap.

I nodded in the affirmative. Sharing a bowl of Oregon's finest hemp after a hearty breakfast was one factor in my state of mind. Regardless, it doesn't take long for me to become one with a trout stream.

The second evening's dinner consisted of a plate-sized slab of pork steak that Rick grilled over propane flame. Canned peaches were a last-minute addition to the menu after our delicatessen macaroni salad lost its flavor overnight. A delicate hint of dead animal on my steak begged for a splash of Heinz 57 sauce and reminded how much I missed cooking over wood coals. When I asked how pork steak became a tradition, Rick replied, "Dusty liked it the first time I prepared it, so that's what we eat."

The brief exchange confirmed that, more often than not, good enough sets the performance standard for camp cooking. Another interpretation could be my brother limited his complaints, if only to ensure less work for him.

The much-anticipated evening rise involved a series of foibles. My first screw-up was forgetting to check for wind knots. This oversight led to me breaking off a huge rainbow upstream of camp. There is no excuse for bringing a large fish to the fly then losing it because of ineptness.

My second major screw-up, also involving knots, could be blamed on shaky hands and fading light. I positioned a Yellow Stone against a background of sun-bleached bunchgrass and darkening sky hoping to achieve contrast. I rubbed my eyes and squinted, convinced that either excess lacquer or wrapping thread had compromised entry of leader. To complicate matters, the fly's rubber legs dangled to confuse when I turned the shaft of the hook for a good angle. I was reminded that aging rock stars turn deaf and boxers end up punch-drunk. The first thing to go for fly fishers is their eyesight.

Nonetheless, the tippet was inserted into the eye of the hook and a clinch knot consummated in time for me to jog upriver guided by the light of a quarter moon. Slipping into position next to a clump of poison oak, I flipped a short cast to where strong current back-eddied beneath overhanging alder. No sooner did my offering splash on the surface when a huge trout rose to suck it down. Unfortunately, my elation was short-lived. The tippet broke at the first knot, leaving the trout with a hairy lip and me with hurt feelings. As a calf roper, I would have been eliminated in the first round.

With a campfire ban in force, the evening's entertainment consisted of watching bats flit silently through the outstretched branches of tall juniper. After Dusty and I crawled into our tent, I lay on my back and pondered unrequited strikes. Dusty clicked on his headlamp to read. Some time around midnight, the constant splash of the river quenched the sound of chirping crickets and I fell asleep.

DAY THREE

The first hint of an approaching freight train, in this case one that passed a stone's throw from my head, was a hollow echo – like a military helicopter moving slowly over a ridge. The omnipresent sound was followed by a far-off clatter of steel-on-steel, a subtle vibration too unfamiliar to initiate defense. A thousand steel wheels screamed a warning cry when they embraced steel tracks loosened with missing spikes. As the train got closer, ground shook, bright light penetrated darkness and the night monster pounced as if fueled by savage thunder. The noise magnified and reverberated when it bounced off the sheer basalt cliff opposite our once peaceful campsite. Then just like that, the train chugged past and the music of the river took over.

Regarding myself as moderately resilient, I rearranged my pillow (actually a sweatshirt, extra underwear, and socks stuffed into a T-shirt) and settled down, assuming the worst was over. Unfortunately, two more freight trains blasted past before the sun rose over the ridge. The only redeeming part of a relatively sleepless night was the brilliant star show that took over the night sky when I got up to relieve the dull ache in my bladder.

I am no wimp. I played football in high school, which required having fair tolerance for both giving and receiving crushing blows to the head, shoulders, and legs. I have endured sharp pain induced by a dentist's sadistic probe into sensitive gum tissues. I ski on knees crippled with missing cartilage without the aid of pain-killing drugs. But having your auditory senses repeatedly crushed by a fast-moving train when you are locked in deep sleep is different. The BNSF experience produced a hangover exceeded only by drinking rotgut whiskey paired with 50-cent cigars. I could barely crawl out of my sleeping bag. My shoulders felt as if a professional wrestler had torn off both arms. Crusty tear ducts and nasal passages packed with campground lint added to the torment.

The act of frying bacon provided solace, however. The sizzle and pop of bacon cooking on medium heat is soothing. Bacon was the one luxury meat my parents indulged when I was a youngster. Mom entrusted me to instruct the butcher on thickness of cut, make sure he didn't put his thumb on the scale, and deliver the product home – all wrapped in sturdy Kraft paper. Back then I honed my culinary talents on an electric range. It's a completely different scenario to fry up a raft of bacon over a cranky gas flame. A particular challenge that morning on the Deschutes involved irregular-shaped bacon slices with twisted grain that caused them to behave like kindergarteners refusing to lie still at naptime. *Don't crowd them.* I told myself. *Let them express their individuality. Tame the sizzle.* I manage bacon slices with a fork because using a spatula is like flock shooting. You can't home into a target. Despite operating in a compromised state, I made love to each slice of bacon, carefully changing their position to match the contour of the frying pan, and retaining grease only as necessary to eliminate the need for safety glasses.

Cooking a perfect slice of bacon is a cerebral experience

similar to toasting a marshmallow golden brown over wood coals. Both tasks require your total attention. It's also possible that you get high from what organic chemists term the "Maillard reaction," where sugars react with amino acids during thermal breakdown of bacon fat to produce an intoxicating aroma. I know dogs are attracted to the odor of frying bacon. Most people are too.

While the frying pan cooled to touch, I munched on a hot piece of bacon to chase the wool rug taste from my mouth and drained grease onto an editorial page of the *Oregonian*. A disparaging headline, "To Keep America Strong, We Must Defeat Osama, Obama and Chelsea's Mama," was not shared with Rick. I had no desire to wind him up over politics after spending the previous evening sharing disparate views on reincarnation. Meanwhile, a trio of blue rental rafts packed with day-trippers in orange Type B life vests passed by. A particularly buxom lass led the pack, resplendently outfitted in a red bikini top. Her long blonde ponytail and 10-gallon white cowboy hat complimented remarkable cleavage. *What would it be like to wrestle with her in an oversize sleeping bag?* I imagined.

After breakfast dishes were washed, Dusty and Rick hiked to the nearest outhouse, which by my calculation was two miles down the railroad tracks. I feigned temporary blockage, too ashamed to admit that I had hidden in the brush to deal with a gastric cramp that came upon me like a thief in the night. Left on my own, I fished a series of side pools that produced two hefty 16-inchers. Another slab-sided male back-flipped at the sting of the hook after I coaxed him from the shelter of a huge boulder. Rick would never know that I allowed my fly to drift deep to entice a strike.

Transferring my knowledge from Blue Mountain streams I

was familiar with to the Deschutes became mostly a matter of scale. In both scenarios, current pattern, depth, and structure dictated where trout lay. Fish were found where deep water, turbulent flow, and large boulders provided cover. They resided in feeding lanes formed on outside bends of the channel and they lurked near current edges where insects fell from overhanging vegetation. Divergent current seams and complex eddies that pushed insects to the bank were favored, as were swirls or collection spots where current swelled over submerged boulders. The largest trout showed at low light. Or maybe they were there all along.

Testing all angling theory, I clambered along a shot-rock slope next to the railroad tracks until poison oak blocked my progress. Overhead sun glared off the water, making fish skittish, so I hiked back to camp where I found a place in the shade to nap. The desire to feel cool water on my legs then led me to leave my waders hanging on a juniper branch. It wasn't until I hiked past a small group of guided anglers that a notion struck home: *I am a trout bum. Not the troubadour, gonzo fly fisher that author John Gierach once described, but a fly fisher who looked like a bum.* My gear vest flapped open to expose a sunburned chest. I wore a sweat-stained "Titlist" ball cap that hid a receding hairline and my zip-leg nylon shorts looked like they came out of a Goodwill bargain bin. The only thing that distinguished me from a lost hobo was a custom-made fly rod.

In stark contrast to my pedestrian attire, the river shoreline was thicker than fleas with anglers dressed like they stepped out of an Orvis catalog. It was a virtual parade of Patagonia outerwear, a testimonial to certain dress codes that predominate on iconic western rivers supporting guide services and anglers wealthy enough to pay for the privilege of having someone row, cook, and, if necessary, cast for them.

Avoiding yet another nasty patch of poison oak, I crossed a sagebrush-dotted flat. Two anglers tossed nymphs on the Reservation shore. An adult bald eagle, chased by a mob of crows, soared high above the river. I methodically worked a lengthy stretch of fast-moving water punctuated with washtub-sized boulders. My reward was one small rainbow trout. The result was frustrating, but the thing was, I knew trout were there. They may have been spooked from my presence or had a sore mouth from being caught before, but they were there.

Complacent trout were not the only issue. My daily battle with poison oak had transitioned from inconvenience to crisis. An allergic reaction that began with a few scattered pimples had spread to a flock of oozing nodules the size of a grain of rice. Both ankles were affected, as was the inside of my right thigh. The crook of my left thumb also throbbed where I had brushed a poison oak branch aside. Scratching provided passing relief, but worsened the condition. A warm washrag applied to my itch produced an orgasmic rush, where joy competed with pain. It was like dancing with the devil! I'd been through the experience enough to know my only choice was to ride things to the final stage or until the affliction resembled an angry red burn. I'll never forget a poison oak outbreak that occurred during my honeymoon summer on the Rogue River. Desperation led me to seek relief with an old school remedy that involved soaking intimate body parts in steaming hot bathwater amended with a quart bottle of Pine Sol.

While I played off the evils of poison oak, Dusty contemplated two horned toads that found reward with the bountiful stonefly hatch. He shared that a robust-bodied toad (assumed to be female) pounced on a giant red stonefly that ventured too close. As if to celebrate the moment, a leaner toad of the opposite gender (inferred) crawled over to demonstrate a series of exaggerated pushups, proving that males will do anything to impress. When I returned to camp, the pair rested side by side on a flat rock near our fire pit. The robust toad rested her right "hand" on the skinny one's posterior to create a pleasant domestic scene.

Over my last can of PBR, I confessed that I had missed far more fish than I hooked. "I don't understand how so many big trout pounced on my oversized foam-body fly only to come up empty," I said. "Is it because high-density synthetic material resists the buccal force a trout imparts at the moment of take?"

Unimpressed with the faux science behind my theory, Dusty came up with a more practical explanation. "Maybe they're trying to knock the stonefly out and take it down to the bottom of the river where they can pin it against a rock and chew the wings off."

One thing was for sure though, Deschutes River redbands were far more wary than Blue Mountain trout that I was familiar with. They were wary of drift boats and rubber rafts that drifted past or tethered over their resting places. They were wary of the constant traffic of fly fishers that populated the shoreline. They were wary of small pieces of hairy foam with dangling hooks. Wary, that is, until twilight, when they lined up in locations that appeared empty at high noon. At twilight, Deschutes River trout appeared to abandon their senses. And twilight is when we elevated our game.

I announced plans to revisit the place of a previous debacle, this time armed with a fresh fly and a well-tied knot. Rick opted to hike up the railroad tracks to his favorite stretch upstream of Whitehorse Rapids. Dusty chose to close his chapter at the "caddis hole." My brief foray produced a thick-bodied 15-incher in the first pool and a silver-sided 13-incher in the second. When I returned to camp to brag, Dusty and Rick were absent, so I headed downstream while I could still see the back of my hand.

I quickly hooked a strong fish that ran to mid-river. Hoping it was the trophy rainbow I had been hoping for, I chased it downstream in fading light, grasping onto boulders, poison oak, and alder to maintain my balance in thigh-deep current. *This lunker isn't going to get off*, I vowed. Aided by a large back-swirl, I gained line and worked the fish close. Unfortunately, my mythical 20-incher turned out to be a foot-long trout snagged in the adipose fin. "Another lazy hook set," my friend Geoff would have said.

Not to be denied, I kept on fishing. Striving for an indeterminate number of last casts is the creed of every successful angler. I hooked an aggressive trout that jumped wildly into a clump of reed canary grass before it broke free and topped the evening off with a fat 16-incher that hammered a Golden Stone drifted along the bank. A quick recap of the evening showed seven trout hooked and landed in less than an hour. It was the kind of action I had only imagined before the trip.

DAY FOUR

Based on my experience camping adjacent to railroad tracks, I would not make a good hobo. The last night at Frenchy's camp was spent hunkered down in the tent as if preparing for mortal combat. Every time I nodded off, yet another freight train raced by to shatter the stillness of the night. Not until dawn broke did I slip into the twilight of my mind, waking up facedown with the sun high in the sky. My head throbbed and both arms had gone "to sleep." The situation had the 1938 anti-war novel, "Johnny Got His Gun," written all over it. *Did my arms get amputated in the night?* I had previous experience reviving a blood-deprived arm with the able assistance of a "live" arm, but never before had both arms been reduced to bags of sand. To make matters worse, my eyelids were crusted shut and I had a kink in my neck. The poison oak rash on my thigh burned as if held to a blowtorch. After my arms came out of their coma, I rolled over on my back to complain about the conductor blowing the train whistle. Dusty looked up from his book and said matter-of-factly, "Maybe he saw a wild animal on the track."

Reminded that sympathy is a hard commodity to come by, I dragged myself out of the tent and fried up a gill-hooked trout I had kept from the evening before. *Maybe a pan fried trout will cheer me up*, I thought. When I offered a share to Rick, he stared at me like I should know better. When I asked Dusty if he wanted a piece, he replied. "Maybe later."

The thing of it was, given Rick's catch and release creed, Dusty didn't want to rock the boat by doing what he had been doing all of his life; that is, eat a kept trout. Suddenly, I didn't feel good about myself. Peer pressure can do that to you. I tossed the uneaten portion of trout in the brush and vowed to feed the next angling casualty to an osprey.

We broke Frenchy's camp at midmorning and pushed off with eight hours of float in front of us. The trip was winding down, but anticipation of what might come bolstered my mood. After successfully navigating lower Whitehorse Rapids, we stopped at milepost 76 and drew straws for a turn at the outhouse. It's unclear whether the subsequent calming effect on my bowels affected the validity of the controversial wolf observation.

What followed the brief rest stop was a series of travelogues. Entertained by multi-colored geological formations that towered hundreds of feet above the river, we drifted to Davison Flat. Included in a constant-changing panorama of stone were pinnacles, anticlines layered with columnar basalt and rock-studded headlands. Downslope from high elevation hills, bunchgrass-covered benches loomed 300 feet or more above the river.

At North Junction, Rick pointed out features of the destructive 1996 flood, including a massive gravel bar deposited where angry flow T-boned a sheer rock cliff. Other evidence of the historical flow event was newish siding tacked to vintage summer cabins. We floated past a lineup of drift boats parked on the sandy shoreline and gawked at a group of managed anglers on a freshly mowed lawn. The gathering looked suspiciously like a Spey-casting enclave, followed by a catered lunch of grilled duck with plum sauce.

Next up on the dance card was a mama merganser managing a flotilla of ducklings covered in down. One youngster rode mama's back while 16 siblings strung out single file across the width of the river. A pair of kingbirds chased caddisflies over streamside alder. Redwing blackbirds chortled from the cover of reed canary grass. Bank swallows swooped under and over the railroad trestle. My bird-loving mother would have been in seventh heaven.

Rick offered me a turn at the helm when we approached Two Springs Ranch, where the Reservation boundary peels off from the west side of the river. I sensed Dusty's apprehension, but ignored his wild-eyed look too eager to try my hand at commanding a raft to worry about his feelings. Rick's only advice before trading seats was, "row away from trouble." I struggled early on to find the sweet spot between competing boulders, once rubbing bottom while I traversed a small rapid. Another time, tricky currents sucked the raft against a shoreline armored with sharp-edged boulders. I got better with practice though. My experience paid off at Buckskin Mary, a Class III rapid, prior to which Rick offered to blindfold Dusty. It was here where I successfully navigated a wave train (a series of large standing waves) that formed where river flow became pinched between narrow bedrock formations to drop 50 feet in elevation over a distance of less than a football field.

Dusty spelled me briefly to row workman-like through a long flat stretch where upriver winds blew us sideways, reminding that fully loaded rubber rafts operate like a sailboat. A relentless sun bore down on our sunburned bodies as we floated past a never-ending display of rock formations. Campgrounds sprouted up every few miles, interspersed with long stretches of shoreline lined with signs that shouted, "No Trespassing." An SUV kicked up dust on the right-bank access road gated to all but members of the exclusive Deschutes River Club. The sighting caused Rick to give the middle finger to the next "Private Property" sign.

Rick took over like a designated hitter when we approached the gatekeeper's house at milepost 62 to row the final five miles. Reaching a popular stretch favored by thrill-seeking weekend rafters, we blasted through roller coaster chutes at dangerous Wapinitia, bounced off fractured basalt and navigated Box Car – a Class IV rapid that includes a 20-foot vertical drop and a "suck hole."

The float trip ended without further fanfare at the Maupin City Park, where we unloaded and headed to *The Oasis* café for a traditional cheeseburger and chocolate shake. Afterwards, we held hands in the parking lot and sang "Kum ba yah" (just kidding). When I thanked my companions for the trip, Dusty looked me in the eye and said, "We do it every year."

Any confusion as to the true meaning of our exchange could be attributed to poor communication between brothers. Regardless, I took his comment as an invitation to return. It's possible my behavior was deemed good enough to become part of the permanent agenda. If in doubt, consider what transpired after Rick demonstrated his culinary skills with pork steak.

Back to that wolf: several email exchanges with the Western Species Conservation Defenders of Wildlife and the Oregon Department of Fish and Wildlife failed to provide sufficient evidence to confirm my sighting at milepost 76. Even the part about pups yelping from a remote den refused to convince interested parties I knew what I was talking about. After flunking questions about broadness of snout, paw size, and how the canine held its tail, I know what to look for next time.

A state wildlife biologist politely assured me that our sighting was most likely a feral dog. "I hope my report doesn't get placed in the same file as a Bigfoot sighting," I replied.

The biologist laughed, but the joke was on me. Being reminded you are a novice is never a positive experience.

I still maintain a wolf ran down that steep hillside, though I also admit to recently seeing a malamute mix on a leash that looked remarkably similar. In any event, and half a dozen float trips later, the "Call of the Wild" experience at milepost 76 remains as firmly entrenched in my mind as the near-drowning episode at Oh Shit Rock is for Dusty. Big trout, freight trains in the night, poison oak, magnificent columnar basalt, and learning something new about myself also come to mind.

Cookies, Rattlesnakes, and Bears

A MUCH-ANTICIPATED FLOAT TRIP on northeastern Oregon's Wallowa River started off with Ken admitting that he left a bag of fresh-made cookies on the kitchen counter. "How many did you make?" Ted asked.

"Sixty. They're chocolate chip," Ken replied.

We were 15 minutes down the road. I did the math and turned my truck around. Losing out on 20 cookies apiece is not something to be taken lightly.

The four-day float trip was on me. "He who chooses, drives," I was told at the Gaslight Tavern where we discussed menu and other logistics. Admittedly, I'd been mesmerized by a presentation that Grant Richey, owner/guide of the Minam Store, gave to our fly caster club. Ted, Ken, and I had twice floated roadside sections of the Grande Ronde River in pontoon boats, but those outings did not involve overnight camping. Sharing breathing space in a small tent tends to create more drama than arm wrestling over who gets the top bunk in a rental cabin.

The Wallowa River joins up with the Minam River at the unincorporated town of Minam. The first 10 miles of float parallel the Wallowa-Union railroad track. After the Grande Ronde River combines its flow near Rondowa, canyon walls close in and deep bedrock-lined pools are more common than long riffle-runs. Talus slopes, basalt lava caves, and unique geologic features that include "rooster combs" and "devil's postpiles" intrigue. Dense stands of old-growth fir and ponderosa pine line a river corridor that opens up to expose wind-swept slopes and pioneer homesteads for the remaining 29 miles of Wild & Scenic River.

Recreational rafting is a major draw to this roadless area. Class I and II rapids are the norm, leading to few technical challenges for experienced boaters. Thrill-seeking rafters push off from the Minam Store in late spring when peak runoff from snowmelt occurs. More interested in fishing, we timed our late June float trip to coincide with a declining hydrograph and reduced competition for shoreline campsites. In anticipation of an early summer hatch, fly boxes were stuffed with dries.

Our leisurely drive began in sagebrush country. We traveled south to Wallula Junction and east up the Walla Walla River valley to be greeted by black-soil fields of alfalfa, wheat and peas. Two more hours of driving time and we crested the Blue Mountains at Tollgate. A brief stop in Elgin for a burger and the purchase of a 12-pack of Rainier "pounders" put us in the Minam Store parking lot by early evening. Our homey two-bedroom suite afforded a peek at the river. Cooking and food storage involved an ancient General Chef combination stove/refrigerator with topside gas burners. Interior walls of tongue-and-groove knotty pine and a water-stained fiberboard ceiling reminded me of my circa 1910 boyhood home. One bedroom had a double bed and the other a pair of twins. Hand-knotted quilts with a western theme covered marshmallow-soft mattresses.

To ensure the trip did not start off with conflict, I invented a game to sort out sleeping arrangements. "We'll use sugar packets supplied to sweeten our morning cup of coffee as drawing cards," I said to my two dubious-looking pals. When they didn't argue, I wrote 1A, 1B, and 2, respectively, on individual packets and placed the trio of "cards" in a Styrofoam cup. Ted drew 2, the double bedroom. I drew 1A and chose the twin bed closest to the bathroom. By default, Ken ended up in the single bed against the back wall. The outcome was not challenged because Ted had reserved the suite on his charge card and he snored.

Rather than test the evening rise, we sat on the front porch stoop, sipped Rainiers, and watched long-eared bats circle silently overhead. Ted surprised us by pulling out a joint that someone gave him ("Girl Scout Cookie" brand, as I recall). We passed the joint around and watched a large moth drop from the roof and spin around the gravel walkway. Time passed. The moth lifted off, bounced crazily off the porch overhang, and disappeared into the night. Its chaotic activity spurred a thought. "Ever hear of shivering thermogenesis?" I asked. "It's a term physiologists use to explain how moths generate heat to activate their flight muscles before take off."

Neither fishing partner pulled on my interesting thread of moth behavior, leading to a pause in conversation. Ted finally broke the ice by remarking he brought along bear spray "just in case." When the comment failed to elicit a response, he shared looking on Google Earth "to get an idea of what the river looked like."

The latter remark prompted Ken to ask, "How far should we float each day?"

According to the U.S. Bureau of Reclamation's map of the river, the distance from Minam to take-out spanned 38 miles at a gradient drop of approximately 20 feet per mile. Based on a reported discharge of 2,000 cubic feet per second at Troy, we estimated an average float speed of 3 miles per hour. "Without doing the math and allowing for extra time to fish, we need to travel about 10 miles a day," I said.

We retired with fat sassy rainbow trout on our minds. The sandman took over until Ken woke up around 3 a.m. with beer pressing his bladder. Stumbling his way to the bathroom in the dark, he bumped into our bedroom door on the way out and tripped on my footboard on his return trip. "It's darker than shit," he mumbled.

Following an in-room continental breakfast of day-old coconut scones and peach yogurt, we walked over to the river and made ourselves familiar with the 16-foot rental raft. Its 125-gallon Yeti cooler performed double duty as the rower's seat. Non-perishable food items were packed in an aluminum, "bear-proof" dry box and gear bags got strapped down in a convenient nylon mesh net. We each held tight to a rigged up fly rod, anticipating a cast or two during the day's float.

I took position at the oars after Ted announced, "We want to see how it's done."

"Not much to it," I replied, reaching back to my previous experience on the Deschutes River. "You watch for obstacles and row away from danger."

Golden stones and caddisflies flitted over the water's surface, followed by occasional surface action from feeding trout. We passed Minam State Park and floated safely through the first

4 miles of mellow river that included one Class II "roller wave" and a huge boulder that pinched flow in half at House Rock. Ted sat vigilant on the bow, instructing Ken where to cast and directing me where to row. Ken gained enough confidence to take the helm after a short stop to stretch our legs. According to my journal notes, he scraped seven large rocks in the next hour and a half. His best rowing was at Blind Fall Rapids, river mile 5.5. Meanwhile, I hooked and released three nice rainbow trout casting a Royal Wulff from the bow.

"You sure tossed Ken to the wolves," Ted confided, when we stopped for lunch.

"What do you mean?" I replied.

"That was the worse section of river."

"I can't help it if he tried to steer the raft like a pontoon boat. You row a raft backward to control speed and direction in a river, not forward."

I took the oars again before we floated past two gals soaking the bottom half of their bikinis in the river. "How's it going?" we yelled.

"Taking a break from herding cattle," they yelled back. Both women were built in the category of what my brother, Daran, used to call "butcher's cut." That is, plenty of meat on the bone but without extraneous fat.

Farther downstream, near river mile 9, we found a camping spot on a wide gravel bar. A musty odor of busted sod and steer manure hung in the air. It took two failed attempts to erect Ted's tent before we were forced to read the directions. Then we screwed it up again.

Ken fired up the gas grill and served up ½-lb sausage dogs accompanied by a healthy portion of pork-and-beans, after which his chocolate chip cookies came out for the second time that day. When the sun dropped behind the hill, Ken and Ted strung up their rods and cast to a stretch of swift-moving water that flowed evenly from bank to bank. "You're wasting your time. There's no holding areas for trout," I said.

I eventually got bored watching them and stepped in several yards below to swing a No. 6 Royal Stimulator like I might for steelhead. As if by miracle, a large trout hiding along the stream margin struck the fly to shake me from my revelry. A spirited tussle in fast current ensued, after which I eased a slab-sided 18-incher to the shallows for release. "No trout in its right mind, huh?" they chided.

A brief thunder and lightning storm, coupled with torrential downpour, drove us to seek shelter. Ted positioned his sleeping bag against the backside of the tent, which left Ken and I straddling the door in a perpendicular arrangement. "Suits me. I don't need to get up in the night," Ted said, when we asked if he minded that his exit was blocked.

The fact that I'm old school led to them ganging up on me after I stumbled around camp by the light of a waning moon. I felt like a hen with a bloody head; the one that all the other chickens in the coop get their protein fix from. While I fully accept that falling down in the dark is a safety issue, a person should not reject their senses for the sake of convenience in the form of an LED flashlight.

The morning broke with certainty when Ted popped out of the tent and announced. "I want to start off rowing." He surely looked like a river guide in a sea blue, long-sleeve, gingham shirt and matching sun-blocker neck flap cap. I pondered my faded red "Coca Cola" logo T-shirt – not quite the look – and reminded, "Don't row downstream."

A half-mile past camp, the Grande Ronde River met up to

double the flow. Canyon walls pressed close, sheltering us from a relentless sun. Ted mastered the oars in time to successfully "shoot" Sheep Creek rapids at river mile 12. We beached our raft on a wide sandy beach near Clear Creek in late afternoon. Ken stretched the two large trout kept for dinner across a log and filleted them using a technique he had seen on YouTube.

Question: How do you divide up two fish three ways? Answer: cut each filet into three pieces and don't argue about the tail portions.

I fried the filets in hot oil skin-side down and served them with a carrot/broccoli/onion stir-fry that Ted discreetly scraped into the bushes. Lucky for me, the trout was moist and they deemed the accompanying wild rice dish as "okay."

After paper plates were burned and the frying pan was washed, we sipped Bullet whiskey from tin cups and passed around a bowl of Smokehouse almonds and dark chocolate M&Ms. Whomever "bogarted" the snack bowl was casually reminded to "pass it along." Peer pressure is a powerful incentive when properly applied.

I whittled on a piece of driftwood while Ted and Ken speculated what part of my leg might get cut off. "You've got to put the torque to knots," I said, in defense of my aggressive technique. Star gazing and poking at wood coals took over the rest of the evening, suggesting that intellectual conversation is overrated on wilderness fishing trips.

With familiarity comes increased confidence. On the morning of day three, Ken handled the raft like a seasoned guide when we "surfed" through Martin's Misery, the last class II rapid of the float. Unfortunately, fish catching continued to be slow. Trout were either less abundant or harder to catch than we had been led to believe from angler posts on the Internet. Our combined catch was a paltry eight rainbow trout, two redside shiners, and three northern pikeminnow. As Grant Richey later told us, "If you want to catch trout on dries, I suggest you fish the Wallowa."

Operating like a well-trained team now, time taken to erect the tent was reduced to an efficient 15 minutes. Lacking the ability to accept rote instruction from my companions, I was fired from the process. As further punishment, I was relegated to double-bagging daily bowel movements and dismantling the honey bucket.

It was here, on a camp near Green Canyon, where an encounter with dangerous wildlife occurred. Forcing my way through streamside willow, I heard the warning buzz of a rattlesnake. I froze in position, mesmerized by the flicker of its tongue. Then I remembered Ken's sage words: "They can only strike a distance that equates to one-third of their body length."

That gives me a two-foot margin of safety, I thought, moving three steps back and taking careful note of the snake's location. Lacking an advanced degree in wildlife science, visions of snakes that hurl poisonous fangs, quill-shooting porcupines, and being mauled by a bear can populate your mind.

After putting down a plate-size T-bone steak and a half-pound of fried potatoes for dinner, I was reminded of a trip to Ireland. "The Irish don't want you to go home hungry," I said. "Boiled potatoes are served with every meal. Even with fish and chips."

We munched on our daily ration of chocolate chip cookies while Ted once again brought up his concern about bears. Earlier that evening, I shared a macabre story about a guy who encountered a black bear on the trail, got bucked off his horse, and had his head chewed off. Needless to say, the story only increased Ted's angst. He unfolded a sheet of paper kept in his back pocket and read out loud, voice rising in pitch as he worked down a list of safety precautions for campers in bear country:

• Prepare all meals 100 to 200 yards from where you sleep.

• The cook should change clothes after each meal.

• Use unscented garbage bags.

• Keep bear spray in your tent for when someone gets up in the night.

Meanwhile, I kept some thoughts to myself. *"Talk about inconvenient!"* *"Good luck reading the fine print on the can of bear spray prior to use."* Admittedly, I did not understand the depth and complexity of Ted's feelings, most likely because I had spent a lifetime putting danger out of my mind. In contrast, Ken appeared more sympathetic. *Perhaps because Ted shared the pain of Ken's erratic rowing on day one?* I wondered.

I am often reminded that camping trips with fishing buddies reinforce differences, such as the type and amount of libation consumed, what constitutes a well-balanced meal, the need to share details of a bowel movement, and concern over wild animals in the night. In some ways, fishing buddies are like marriage partners. A certain degree of tolerance and mutual respect is required to maintain a relationship. Not to mention time away from each other. Mostly though, I hoped that my two able companions were half as tolerant of my behaviors as I imagined I was of theirs.

I took the oars for our last morning on the river because I like to row. Ted resumed his observer role because he believes in looking out for others. Ken spent the day casting from the bow because he badly wanted to catch another trout. According to my journal notes, Ken tried 18 different patterns that involved 26 variations over three days of fishing, including Yellow Stimulator, Clouser Minnow, Parachute Adams, Beadhead Hare's Ear,

Pheasant Tail Nymph, Rock Worm, Muddler Minnow, Sculpin, Royal Wulff, Yellow Stone, Triple Renegade, Caddis Fly Larvae, Stonefly Nymph, Beadhead Wooly Bugger, and Purple Lightening Bug.

In contrast, I stayed with the same six trout patterns I knew best. Admittedly, I spent more time dragging a fly behind the raft than casting to potential holding water as a means to manage my ADD.

Dense conifer side slopes eventually gave way to open hillsides covered with bunchgrass and big sage. Our float ended at the Powwatka Bridge, where my dust-covered Tundra was parked. Ignition keys were zip-tied to the undercarriage as informed and the motor turned over on first try (always a concern). A leisurely stop at Boggan's Oasis for chocolate milkshakes was followed two hours down the road for Jason Burgers and beers at the Tuxedo Tavern in Pomeroy.

As for Ken's chocolate chip cookies, the last of them got killed off before we delivered him to his front door. Twenty apiece turned out to be a good round number.

Floating Down Memory Lane

"The guy at Red's said it didn't matter where we put our pontoon boats in," Ken reported. "They've been fishing the entire stretch of the Yakima River from near Cle Elum down to Big Pines Campground."

Ken always calls fly shops for the latest information. That way he doesn't show up ignorant. "That's a polite way of saying they haven't homed into fish," I replied. "It also explains why we only saw one boat on the water in the lower canyon."

"He did say the middle of the day hasn't been good. That they focus on hoot owl time."

In hindsight, I should have known better than to expect a 20-fish day on my first trip for trophy rainbows in the Yakima River Canyon. Contrast my geographic naïveté to Ted and Ken who grew up in nearby Yakima, the "Palm Springs of Eastern Washington." They both chomped at the bit to float down memory lane.

Ted pointed out a dilapidated old building with a faded marquee. "That's the Pomona Tavern," he said. "We used to stop there for a cold one after a day of tubing."

"I don't remember those houses when we were in high school," Ken remarked, when we passed a cluster of ranch-style homes parked halfway up Umtanum Ridge. Next up through the windshield of Ken's truck was a railroad trestle that reminded Ted of a blissful summer day when he hooked a trout at the precise moment a freight train clattered past.

Trying to ignore their nostalgic chitchat, I looked out the side window and studied features of the river. After doing the pontoon boat thing twice with borrowed craft, I was eager to apply my skills in a recently purchased 9-foot, burgundy-and-white "Wilderness" model.

One advantage of getting picked up last on the drive to the launch is you get to pump up your pontoon boat first. This luck-of-the-draw left time for me to chat with a local artist who had set up an easel in the shade of tall cottonwood. I peered over her shoulder as she created, with deft strokes of pastel chalk, an idyllic scene of a river that ran bank full. It was irrigation season, valley orchards were thirsty, and upstream storage reservoirs had released flows that appeared more suitable for rafting than fishing. A constant parade of recreational rafters in neon tank tops and swimsuits, some hosting shade umbrellas, validated this impression.

I pushed my virgin pontoon boat from shore and found that my tiptoes barely touched the water's surface. Coupled with short oars, the feeling was of being "inadequate." *Is my*

swivel seat mounted too high or did I purchase child-size oars?
I thought. *If so, it's too late now.* It soon became evident that
trout had little time to react to my presentation. There are no
comebacks when you toss a fly from a fast-moving vessel in a
river. I cast to a rise or a holding zone and hoped for a strike
before I was transported downriver. While every bend in the
channel presented new opportunity, lost chances began to add
up exponentially.

The other issue was a pontoon boat that acted like a complacent mule. No matter how hard I worked to maintain a desired casting angle, it spun sideways in the wind or twisted in
divergent current. When I dropped my offering into pocket water, line drag ensued. When I slowed my kick, I got sucked toward the bank, where overhanging brush reached out to grab
me. Meanwhile, Ken operated his boat like a ferryboat captain
working riptide. He nimbly worked his oars when shore-to-
shore navigation was required and relied on oversize fins to
move into casting position. When a promising stretch of water
beckoned, he dropped a lead anchor to slow his approach. In
contrast, my mesh bag of rocks rarely held me in place. Then
there was a certain small yellow fly. "I picked up four trout in
that last run and had several hits using this one," he said, after
pulling alongside. "Unfortunately, it's the only one I have."

His small yellow fly consisted of two strips of foam, brown
saddle hackle, and a collar of deer hair. The top strip of foam
was light brown and the bottom bright yellow. "I've got similar
ones," I said, before swapping out three different flies without
a strike. It had been three hours since the last failed hookset
and I needed to catch a fish – if only to prove I could. I was
not frantic though. It was too pleasant of a day to get frantic.
Desperate for something good to happen would be an accurate

description of how I felt, though.

Although the afternoon appeared more suited for sun-burning the back of my neck than catching trout, I ramped up my effort. There would be no more mindless backward floats through shallow riffles. No ogling of bikini-clad teenage girls. No watching osprey soar high overhead. No more envy for anglers who cast from the bow of a drift boat while their buddy held position with deft strokes of his oars.

Time had also become too short to scope bunchgrass-lined slopes for chukars and bighorn sheep. My last hour on the river would be devoted to one purpose and one purpose only – to catch a trout. I tied on my go-to fly, a No. 10 Yellow Stimulator, and worked the shoreline with my bantam fins and tiny oars like there was no tomorrow. I focused on the outside margin of bends in the channel, where oxygenated current pushed food to waiting trout. I cast to where rock rubble and sunken logs provided cover and where overhanging brush shaded. I worked current edges, pocket pools, and back-eddies where flecks of foam collected. I managed my line to extend the float and sometimes deepen the drift of my fly. Despite due diligence and attention to detail, not a single trout was brought to the fly.

The 10-mile float ended at Red's Fly Shop where cold brews beckoned. Ken attempted to share details of his catch from position at the middle barstool, but the topic died on the vine because Ted and I had nothing to add. Being reminded of your incompetence is not high on any fly fisher's list.

"One guide mentioned that trout were eating grasshoppers," I said, "but I never saw a single hopper fall into the water."

"He told me to cast into the reed canary grass and let my hopper pattern slide into the water," Ken replied. "Supposedly fish snug up to the bank waiting for something edible to drop in."

"All I know is I tossed hopper patterns and big MF hairy flies to the stream margin all day long," I replied. "The one small trout I caught struck a Renegade that I left dangling on the surface when I rowed with my rod in the holder. I didn't see a single adult caddis or stonefly and only an occasional midge. In other words, there was little incentive for trout to rise to a fly."

I studied the bottom of my glass of Red Hook Ale and listened to Ken and Ted debate the length of time that grasshoppers float before they sink to their death. Unfortunately, neither found a hopper to toss into the river as a test of their respective theory.

One thing we all shared in common, however, was chasing grasshoppers as a kid. "Yellow wings were the big ones," Ken said. "We'd tie a loop of sewing thread to the crease between their head capsule and pronotum and fly them like a kite. When they quit flying, we'd jerk their head off."

"I bet you didn't use fancy words like 'pronotum' back then," I said.

"Yeah. It would have been more like crack behind their head," he admitted, before adding, "Sometimes I shot them with my BB gun or slingshot."

"Things kids did before WiFi and video games," Ted chimed in.

"I wasn't as sadistic," I said. "My favorite pastime was packing them in glass Mason jars and harvesting their spit as tobacco juice."

Ted's dark side was revealed after he swigged the last of his Black Butte Porter and shared, "I might have burned them with a magnifying glass."

It could have gone on like that all evening, except we had to hit the road or face the wrath of our wives. There would be plenty of time to reminisce about days gone by on the drive home.

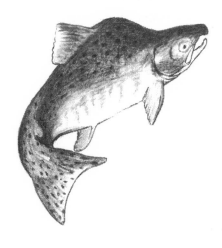

Humpies Aren't Just for Grandkids

Every odd year since 2011, I've commuted from the dry side of Washington State to chase pink salmon or "humpies" (so-called for the distinct hump that males exhibit as they near spawning time) on the Snohomish River with guide friend, Ray. The first trip involved wife Nancy, son Matthew, and his two children, Adam and Annalise (who were 6 and 8 years old, respectively). Nobody wanted to stand by while others tossed half-ounce jigs at splashing salmon, so we all cast at the same time.

I flipped a jig off the aft end of the boat, while the other four lined up along the port gunnel. I recall snagging more pinks than I fair-hooked because of a poor retrieve angle, while Matthew's tall frame provided a distinct advantage over his much shorter competitors. Ray leaned back on the bow, eyes wide open and alert for tiny guided missiles that came his way. Despite close quarters, hook-sets were steady, merriment was high, and complaints were few. Several tangled lines and a hundred errant casts later, eight fresh pinks lay in the bottom of the cooler.

Two years later, when the next big run of pinks came in, Nancy opted out. "Too much competition for space," she said.

Ray picked us up at a roadside launch in his jet boat, avoiding the occasional logjam as we blasted down the river. We had no sooner anchored on a current seam than Adam asked, "What makes salmon jump?"

"It's to loosen their egg sacs prior to spawning," Ray replied.

I bit my tongue. I'd heard various explanations for why migrating salmon show at the surface, including "shake off sea lice" and "look for predators," but not this version. *Is it also true that buck salmon jump to loosen their sperm sacs,* I wondered?

In my opinion, salmon jump without apparent purpose when they get frantic. Close quarters, high densities, and nearness to spawning time trigger a startle response and they break the water's surface. The funny part was Adam didn't really care so much why salmon jumped as he wondered why Ray had instructed us to cast to the shore opposite from all the surface action.

The grandkid's casting had improved significantly from their first trip. It also helped that Ray introduced a different technique to reduce the risk of personal injury: drifting ghost shrimp under a bobber. Already proficient in casting, they took turns spooling line from an open-face reel to stretch out the drift and patiently waited for their bobber to "go down." A dozen pinks were quickly set aside for smoking along with several pounds of roe that I reserved for the fall Chinook salmon fishery back home.

"What was your favorite part of the trip?" I asked Annalise, while Ray filleted our catch. She reflected for a few seconds before replying, "Bonking them."

When yet another big run of pinks arrived, I pledged to catch one on my fly rod. Trip logistics quickly complicated when the other set of grandkids asked to join in the fun. Luckily, Ray agreed to shuttle them in pairs (girls first, then boys) on separate afternoon trips. It was a shirtsleeve day in late August when his jet sled took us away from a crowd of eager anglers that stood on virtually every rock and shoreline opening along the Snohomish River.

Annalise and cousin, Sofia, quickly demonstrated ample prowess with spinning rod and reel to land a couple of pinks apiece. Several hero pictures were taken, after which Adam and Liam jumped in the boat for a turn. The boys got their fix of jerking and reeling and settled down with a foot-long ham-and-cheese and party-size bag of chips. *Finally, time for "Papa D" to sneak in a cast!*

Ray anchored in moderate current opposite the Three Rivers RV Park, well out of casting distance from bank anglers. A fresh school of pinks winked, splashed, and rolled beside the boat. For every pink that showed, a dozen or more lurked below the surface. I put together an 8-weight fly rod purchased for the occasion and tied on a 1/8-ounce BeuMac hot pink Maribou Steelhead jig (key word here is PINK!). The feathered jig swung across the current and fluttered when I juiced up action with a series of short quick pulls. Other times, I let the jig hang languidly behind the boat.

Eventually, I felt a hard pull. My fly line knifed crosscurrent and the drag on my brand-new reel sang. A good-sized salmon took off on a long run and surfaced to shed water on the turn. Several nervous minutes later I led a hump-backed buck alongside the boat to where Ray stood vigilant with the net. Adam and Liam took time out from fighting over the last bag of M&Ms to watch the action.

"Good job, Papa D," they said when Ray dropped the thrashing fish on the bottom of the boat. "You didn't get skunked."

As I recall, landing my first pink salmon on a fly was enough of a thrill that I didn't mind getting out-fished by all four grandkids.

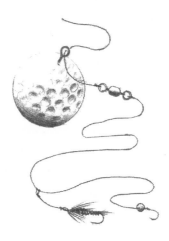

On Beads and Bottlenose

M y l o n g h i s t o r y with mountain whitefish began with a soft take of a No. 12 Renegade that floated where deep current swirled along the exposed root of an old growth fir. According to the Boy Scout handbook, progression to Second Class rank requires that you demonstrate Scout spirit, take an overnight camping trip, pitch a tent, sleep on the ground, and use various rope knots to construct a useful camp gadget. I fulfilled all six of those requirements after hiking down the Coyote Ridge trail to the headwaters of the North Fork, Umatilla River in the summer of 1962. I also landed that big ol' whitefish and a mess of small trout. No matter how hard I search my memory bank though, I don't recall seeing another whitefish rise to the fly since.

Mountain whitefish are native to waters west of the Rocky

Mountains. These large-scaled, adipose-fin cousins to salmon and trout were once abundant enough to be a staple food of the Plateau Indian diet. Captains Meriwether Lewis and William Clark called them "bottlenose," possibly because of a pointy-mouth they use to poke for insect larvae living in rock crevices. Present-day anglers lacking a background in ichthyology have been known to confuse them with native minnows and suckers. My grandchildren drift a No. 18 Prince Nymph for mountain whitefish that school in a rock-lined pool near our family cabin. When the bite slows, a juicy caddisfly or stonefly larvae might be added to the hook.

"Can you catch them with a fly?" Ted asked, when I called to inquire if he wanted to chase whitefish on the Hanford Reach of the Columbia River.

"Sure you can. Glow Bug and Orange Hackle patterns work. One difference is I use spinning tackle to keep my offering on the bottom."

"I'm bringing a fly rod loaded with sink tip line," Ted replied. "What you're doing ain't fly fishing."

Evolving ethics aside, I stayed with a faux "Rocket Red" Exude egg slipped above the shank of a No. 10 bait hook and drifted deep with the aid of a terminal slinky weight. *Some days you need to catch a fish if only to prove that you can.* I filled the boat cooler with a smoker-load of fat whities while Ted gripped his fly rod without a single take. He claimed to have once felt the pull of a whitefish, but my guess is he hooked a patch of milfoil based on what he reeled in.

The Hanford Reach is home to mountain whitefish year round. The Washington State record, a robust 5 1/8-pounder, was taken near Vernita Bar in 1983. I drag a small spinner from my boat to entice a strike in the heat of summer and angle for them in the coldest part of winter using an Orange Hackle fly tipped with a maggot. Whitefish are easiest to catch, however, when large schools gather on fall Chinook salmon spawning grounds to gobble up loose eggs.

When the next November rolled around, I checked in with Leroy since we hadn't fished together for a while and he likes to catch "Mr. White" as much as I do. "I'll bring my boat and pick you up at your front door," I wrote in an email. "Whitefish should be looking for their annual protein fix about now."

"As far as the whites go," he replied. "I'm afraid I must decline. They are probably done eating eggs and may not be where we last found them."

I felt out of sorts. Rejection is difficult to deal with when you offer to do all the work. A sack of donuts may also have been involved. However, I picked myself up off the floor and got back on the phone. Unfortunately, my success rate continued to go downhill. A neighbor begged off – "a bout of standing pneumonia." Another fellow retiree had to take his granddaughter to a doctor appointment. A third friend also declined – "Sorry, can't fit it in."

Then I remembered Ron. He liked all kinds of fishing. As luck would have it, my invitation struck a chord. No sooner did I say the word "whitefish," then he launched into a story about catching a batch of 3-pounders in the Henry's Fork. "If you get a green- or red-colored Copper John near the bottom, a whitefish is almost guaranteed," Ron said. "Some guys like to Czech-nymph, but I prefer to suspend a fly below a Thingamabobber. I've also seen whitefish cruise around in the evening picking off duns, spinners, and emergers."

I didn't share that I had only seen one whitefish rise to a fly and that was over 50 years ago. "We'll be using spinning gear to get our lures down to where the whitefish are," I said, hoping to dissuade him from bringing his fly rod. "Plus, they are keyed into salmon eggs this time of year. I pin a small orange bead or faux egg above a single hook. Alaskan fly fishers use a similar method to entice big rainbows that follow sockeye salmon spawn."

The morning broke chilly with ominous gray clouds, so I nixed the usual 8-mile run upriver from north Richland and trailered my boat to Ringold Springs where we launched in unseasonable high flows. Our destination, the downstream tip of "forked island," was only a two-minute boat ride away. Standing vigilant on the bow, I managed boat direction and drift speed with my bow-mount motor. One pass later, I hooked and landed two plump whitefish on consecutive casts, while Ron rustled through his tackle bag. "What are you doing?" I asked. "I've got all the gear you need."

"I'm looking for a way to attach a golf ball," he said. "I used one for a dropper weight last time I fished for steelhead off the bank and never got hung up once."

"Now what?" I asked an hour later, when I noticed that Ron had given up on his golf-ball technique.

"I tied on a stonefly nymph with a Copper John for a dropper."

"That might work in the summer, but they want eggs this time of year. How many whitefish of mine do you have to net before you switch to something they want?"

Whether shamed or cajoled, Ron rigged up a terminal slinky with a faux egg affixed 2 feet up the line. One cast into swift-moving current and he was quickly into an 18-inch-long whitefish.

Fast forward to another late fall day on the Hanford Reach. The sun shone bright, a gentle breeze blew from the southwest, and a large "V" of Canada geese honked high overhead. Ted and I arrived at Ringold Springs to find a solitary angler casting a spinner downstream of the irrigation canal. This time we arrived prepared to catch whitefish on our fly rods.

"I'm going to start with spinning gear," I told Ted. "But once we find fish, we'll switch to fly rods and try that Thingamabobber trick of Ron's."

Ted did not argue. You could say he was a new man. "I brought my spinning rod also," he said. "I've changed my mind about having to fly fish all the time. I want to catch a fish."

I moved to the bow of my boat to maintain our course in the half-acre patch where whitefish concentrated. Admittedly, I got tangled up more than once while surrounded by trolling motor, foot pedal, anchor, gear bag, and a large coil of rope. "Do you want to keep any whitefish for your smoker?" I asked Ted.

"You bet," he replied. "I've changed my mind about catch and release. I've decided that I like to eat fish."

Fifteen minutes later, three fat whities flopped in the bottom of the cooler. "Time to get out the fly rods," I announced.

The target area lay in moderate current downstream of a gravel bar island. Salmon redds were still visible following their early November spawn. Gear involved 6-weight rods with floating line and 10 feet of leader suspended below a Thingamabobber. The terminal hook was a Glow Bug fly. A second hook, tied 18 inches up the line, held a single faux egg. We pinched on a size 4 sinker to drop the dual-hook arrangement to the bottom.

Looping short casts alongside the boat, we let our offerings float with the current. Evolution of a fly fisherman does not come easy, however. Managing slack line challenged our resolve, as did maintaining boat position in a broadside breeze. As luck would have it, Ted's strike indicator was first to go down. Meanwhile I couldn't close the deal on a brief rash of pull-downs. Two long drifts passed. I had not hooked a fish and wondered about the wisdom of switching to a fly rod. On our third pass through the zone of whitefish, my bobber went down and stayed down. I set the hook and reeled frantically as if it was my first fish ever. A large whitefish pulled hard and flashed as it twisted and turned in shallow water. "Feels like a new state record," I shouted. With some effort I worked my quarry close to find two whitefish on the end of my line. "A double!"

The sun slipped down behind sand dunes that fronted the Hanford shoreline. An occasional scab-back salmon rolled in the shallows. A lone coyote broke the silence with a series of sharp yips. We pulled our stocking caps down tight and called it a day. A dozen whitefish rested in the cooler, enough to fill our Little Chief smokers and be shared with friends and relatives over the holidays.

Some anglers may argue that using a faux egg and a bobber to elicit a strike does not count as fly fishing. However, I have yet to be sent to the end of the buffet line at a fly caster club meeting as penalty for creative angling. While not the same as catching whitefish on the rise, there's something about a bow on your fly rod that provides incentive for me to try the Thingamabobber trick again.

THE PERFECT ROD

IT WAS DAY ONE of the Tri-Cities Sportsman Show and a boisterous crowd was in attendance. Four of us from the Columbia Basin Fly Casters shared an afternoon shift at the club's booth. Another guy named Dennis demonstrated technique at the main fly tying station. John showed a swarm of wide-eyed youngsters how to craft a Wooly Bugger at a side table. Fred stood at the front of the booth, offering up raffle tickets for a chance at a fly rod and a float tube. As we were instructed on arrival, "One ticket for a dollar and three tickets for two dollars, but we would prefer they buy ten tickets for five dollars."

It was Senior Day. Admission was half price for age 65 and older, which meant the majority of attendees were retirees. Clutching bright orange plastic bags handed out as part of the entry fee, grasping hands reached out for freebies. Over 100 different vendors faced off, offering guided fishing trips, bow hunting equipment, solar panels, wildlife art, whitewater rafting, soaps, candles, T-shirts, beef jerky, and bathtub retrofits. Parked alongside our booth was a F-250 Ford pickup on big tires and elevated shocks. A sign in the passenger-side window read, "$65,950. Fully loaded. 10 year payment plan available." A small child played in the bow of an equally over-priced aluminum boat, largely ignored by its mother who messed with a cell phone. The sweet odor of caramel corn wafted in the air.

I looked across the mass of humanity while a loud speaker penetrated the white noise of crowd din to announce the next seminar: "Walleye fishing techniques starts in five minutes."

A young man with ball cap on backwards pushed a double-decker stroller stuffed with give-aways. His dutiful wife followed with a tiny baby in her arms. I watched them pass and did not try to hawk a ticket. Like many conservation-based clubs, ours had made little progress toward shifting club demographics. "Too bad we can't attract younger people or more female anglers," I remarked to the other Dennis. "I encouraged a young woman to join the club, but she was more interested in riding herd on her rambunctious 4-year old than listening to me."

"I fully understand," he replied. "It's tough when you unleash your charms and find the customer unreceptive."

Meanwhile, our open bowl of hard candy required regular filling.

Hoping to catch a passing person's eye, I stepped up to demonstrate a cast with a 5-weight "Three Creek Outfitters" fly rod (retail value $129). Whether good luck or clever marketing, I sold a raffle ticket to a man who imagined the only thing that kept him from taking up the sport was a new fly rod and reel.

Languishing in my success, I took a break to converse with a fellow club member who stopped by to kill time between the Bengal tiger demonstration and Cee Dub's Dutch oven cook-off. Because neither of us had a recent fishing story to share, we discussed the weather, which eventually led to the topic of spring cleaning. "I organized my fishing equipment last weekend and found a 3-weight fly rod I had completely forgot about," I said. "That's the problem when you have too much gear."

Ron shared that he spent the weekend organizing his rod collection. "I had over twenty rods scattered about the garage," he said. "Some were decent, some were scrounged from yard sales, and others were inherited from my Dad, uncles, and cousins. I also had accumulated sixteen fly lines of unknown weight or manufacture. Some of the rods and lines were over fifty years old."

"From back in the days when you didn't know the difference between weight forward, fast sink, and floating line," I replied.

"And when your tippet was a length of mono from a 200-yard spool," Ron said. "Anyway, I decided to conduct an experiment to see which combination of rods and lines worked best. I established criteria that included casting accuracy, distance, and ease of delivery. I selected five modern graphite and one ancient fiberglass fly rods and six different lines. Each rod was tested with each line to see which combination worked the best for a total of seventy-two tests."

I was impressed. Selling raffle tickets went on the backburner until I got to the heart of his story.

"What's funny was my $15 Ace Hardware fiberglass rod, circa 1950, rated third," he continued. "I decided to keep it as a backup to the two graphite rods that rated highest. Many of the rods and several worn and cracked lines went to the Goodwill."

"That's interesting," I said. "I have seen fiberglass rods advertised as having desired characteristics for certain types of fishing. Like deep-sea trolling, where you need a rod with backbone, but having the flexibility to tire trophy-size fish. I've also read that professional bass anglers prefer glass rods to throw crankbaits. Some fly fishermen say the slow action and deeper flex of a glass rod leads to a more delicate presentation, similar to bamboo. In other words, different kinds of blanks are perfect for certain situations."

"Fiberglass is cheaper," Ron replied.

"I wouldn't use that as a reason to argue for regular use though," I said. "I'd emphasize characteristics like improved balance, comeback rate, and control. You're not likely to purchase a glass Spey rod. It would cast like a flagpole. Graphite is known to be lighter, stronger, and better for distance casting."

But Ron was not to be dissuaded from finishing his story despite my frequent interruption. Anything I added to the conversation merely stretched out his conclusion. "There's a sad ending," he continued, as if I hadn't spoken a word. "I leaned the fiberglass rod against the wall in the garage while I organized the rest of my gear. Then a gust of wind blew it over and my wife backed over it in the car."

I struggled to find the right words to express my sympathy. "That is a sad tale," I said, wiping a rush of tears from my eyes. The finale, while quick and merciful, was sadder than sad. It was a tragedy of great proportion. What could have been a tale of perseverance, redemption, and triumph of spirit turned into a tale of woe when his "top three" fiberglass rod was rendered obsolete. Struck down without a chance to reaffirm its rightful place on the stream.

Stepping back from youngsters wearing paper antlers who

grabbed for the club's candy bowl like it was Halloween, I leaned the raffle fly rod against the back façade of our booth. Given proper care and handling, it could be the perfect rod for an aspiring fly fisher willing to fork over a measly buck for a chance at the winning ticket.

BURY ME with my fly rod

SINGLE MALTS, GHILLIES AND SEA TROUT

MY FIRST VISIT TO THE LAND of castle ruins, single-malt whisky, and "Sea Trout" (the anadromous form of brown trout) took place in 2000 when a main goal was to play golf at The Old Course in St. Andrews. The excursion was largely a work-related boondoggle wrapped around a four-day fisheries conference in Aberdeen. My only participation in the scientific event, except for evening functions where I ate haggis, danced the highland fling, and sampled local single-malts, involved a poster paper that I left tacked up on the back wall of the University of Aberdeen dining hall. Before and after the conference, Nancy and I scanned Loch Ness for "Nessie," learned that you order "whisky" not "Scotch" in the land of the Scots, and played links golf on four different seaside courses.

One thing to understand about Scotland is there are few places where you can stop by the side of the road and wet a line without risk of being arrested by a local conservation officer. The standard angling arrangement for visitors from afar is to book a trip with a ghillie. In other words, you pay for both the company of a guide and the privilege to fish on private property.

Halfway into the trip, I found opportunity to cast on the River Tay near where Beatrice Potter found inspiration for Peter Rabbit, Jeremy Fisher, and Miss Tiggie Winkle, among other irreproachable woodland characters. To facilitate my day on the river, I booked a night at the Dunkheld House Hotel. This four-star country house is located in Perthshire on 280 acres and oversees a mile-and-a-half-long "beat" that includes 17 named pools. Their local ghillie feigned surprise when I arrived at the appointed time (a gentlemanly 9:00 a.m.) because he had double-booked me. "There's not enough room in my boat for two anglers and you'd only waste your money given low water conditions," he said.

The above dialogue is a rough version of his heavy Gaelic tongue. Truth be told, translation required several back-and-forth exchanges. But I was not so easily dissuaded. Rather than sip Earl Gray tea with Nancy in the hotel drawing room, I unpacked my four-piece travel rod and cast Pacific Northwest trout patterns to a dark-colored "Salmon" (also known as an Atlantic salmon kelt or "black"), and the occasional rise of a "Brownie" or resident brown trout.

A more recent trip took Nancy and I to the west coast of Scotland, where I had reserved a tee time to play Royal Troon, site of the 2016 Open. I'd dreamed of teeing off on Hole #8, aptly named "Postage Stamp," a short par 3 with a tiny green surrounded by five treacherous sand bunkers, since I was a youngster. (I'm not telling my score.) Day four of the trip was to be devoted to fishing on the River Snizort, considered as "the most celebrated spate river on the Isle of Skye." The River Snizort is host to Salmon, Sea Trout, and Brownies. Salmon and Sea Trout move up and down the river year round, depending on flood tides, while wild Brownies abound throughout. The main run of Salmon occurs around the first of July and fish continue to migrate into the river until the season closes in mid-October. According to the website, skyesalmon.co.uk, 200 or more Salmon are landed during a good year. Fishing is catch and release.

Nancy and I arrived in early September. Following an overnight flight from Seattle via Iceland that involved lost luggage, we drove north from Glasgow on busy A85. We regaled in the gurgling "burns," misty "glens," and craggy "bens" of Glen Coe, before arriving at touristy Fort William in late afternoon. Shopping for sheep wool sweaters and eating steak pie filled the void until an airport courier arrived with our suitcases. With three hours of driving in front of us, time was running short. Postcard views of the peaks of Glen Shiel, Eilean Donan Castle, and the Skye Bridge were far too brief. It also didn't help when I turned right instead of left at the junction of Dunvegan/Uig and ended up deep in sheep country. Blame my confusion on which side of the road to drive on when entering a roundabout and road signs printed in Gaelic. Needless to say, the sun had dropped below the north Atlantic and our nerves were frazzled when we arrived at the Skeabost House Hotel. Following a welcome change in clothes, kitchen staff rustled up a "wee bit of scran" for our dinner.

To mitigate for me ditching Nancy, I had booked upscale accommodations. The Skeabost House Hotel is an exclusive woodland property built by Lachlan Macdonald in 1871 as a family hunting lodge and converted into a hotel in the 1920s. For 298 quid a night (double occupancy; garden double), we had a view of the sea loch estuary and a 9-hole pitch-and-putt golf course. Dark oak paneling milled from local lumber, luxury bedroom décor, access to over 40 single-malt whiskies, and impeccable service from uniformed staff came with the two-night package.

My fishing day began all by my lonesome in the breakfast dining area while Nancy slept to shake loose eight hours of jet lag. An attractive hostess dressed in a white lace frock and black skirt managed a breakfast buffet of cold cuts, local cheeses, oatmeal, and croissants. The ambience of white tablecloths, crystal drink glasses, high back Windsor cushion chair, Tartan wool rug, and soft pop/jazz background music was largely wasted on me because of gas cramps I attributed to the previous evening's smoked vegetable soup.

I asked the indifferent hostess about the weather. "It could go either way." And if she knew whether I would be fishing from a boat or the bank. "I don't know." Following a hasty visit to the hallway "loo," I quizzed the front desk clerk, who was more informative. I learned that my ghillie, Derek Dowsett, "stocked the river with Salmon" and "a twenty-two pound Salmon was caught this spring." The clerk also shared that it had rained the last few days. "Rain will help," he said. "You will fish from the bank. The river is small."

Trying to suppress my burgeoning excitement, I strolled down a narrow wooded lane to the ghillie's office. I knocked on the door that fronted the river and entered a mudroom with a low ceiling. "Anybody home?" I called out.

A voice from another room replied, "In here!"

Dowsett was gray-bearded, bespectacled, and displayed a wry smile that eased my angst. He sat at a dark oak desk covered with neat stacks of paper and various sized notepads. A laptop computer turned on to an Internet site and a package of Amber Leaf smoking tobacco within easy reach completed the scene. Several whistles on lanyards hung from a hook on the ceiling. Dark wood paneling was peppered with photographs of anglers, rugby events, colorful seabirds, Salmon, and more Salmon.

Owner of Three Esses Ltd., Dowsett is a true "river keeper." Along with overseeing hatchery operations that release up to 10,000 Salmon fry a year, he leases eight quality miles of river, and owns a 35-kW Archimedes screw turbine installed within a 90-year old stone building just downstream of his office. Known as the "old turbine house," the Fort Skeabost hydro once held an aged Frances turbine that supplied electricity to the Macdonald country house.

I sat in a small sofa chair and made small talk while we waited for a second angler to show, all the while hoping that I would not get bumped or have to share water. "Bob is from Texas," Dowsett said. "He fished with me two years ago and got the bug."

The price of a half-day fishing permit was 30 quid, or approximately $50. Another 70 quid bought me Dowsett's able companionship. Arriving without gear of my own, I was loaned knee-high rubber boots, a quality 7/8-weight, 11-foot, one-hand fly rod, and half a dozen unfamiliar-looking flies.

Inner calm had progressed to anxious by the time Bob showed up. He was short in stature and thoughtfully dressed in waterproof clothing, ankle-high rubber boots, brown pocket vest, and a cotton Safari hat. His explanation for late arrival was brief, "Turned down a lane and came to a gate."

"Do you have flies?" Dowsett asked, eager to get on the river.

I'd never held an Atlantic Salmon fly in my hand, but was familiar with patterns shown in fly-tying books in my personal library. I'd also read stories about the Maramichi River of New Brunswick, Canada, where anglers cast flies with colorful names like Black Ghost, Mickey Finn, and Rusty Rat. Most Salmon patterns are not all that different from traditional 20th century steelhead flies. However, more recent fly-tying styles for West Coast steelhead tend to favor gaudy, oversized patterns such as Intruder, Popsicle, and Egg Sucking Leech – the theory being to trigger an aggressive strike rather than giving steelhead something familiar to eat.

Bob pulled several small plastic envelopes from his jacket pocket, each containing a single fly. Some appeared to be nymph patterns, near as I could tell after peeking over his shoulder. "I used this one when I was here before," Bob said, holding up an unexceptional-looking orange-hackle streamer.

Dowsett declared that fly and another "okay" and selected two more from the box on his desk. "You owe me 3 quid for these. That gives you four flies. Should be enough to get you through the day."

Meanwhile, I chilled my jets and wondered if time waiting in the ghillie office counted against my 4 hours of fishing.

"Here's the guy you need to apologize to for being late," Dowsett said, pointing to me by way of introduction. Bob did not acknowledge my presence nor apologize so I made him ride in the overloaded back seat of Dowsett's extended cab pickup to get even.

Dowsett drove us upriver a half-mile or so and parked next to an 18th Century cemetery. The expansive view of a small river meandering through a gentle sloped valley provided a sense of calm. Moss-covered stone fences, farmhouses with gray slate roofs, and distant swales filled with oak trees added to the charm. Green pastures of knee-high grass dotted with white sheep extended in all directions. As Dowsett later shared, "the absentee Scottish lairds put out sheep everywhere where once cattle and the occasional goat grazed alongside cereal crops."

Salmon fishing on the River Snizort is divided into twelve beats, each having a named pool. Beat 1, Ghillie's Pool, is the most downstream location. The numerical arrangement progresses sequentially upstream to Beat 12, Hill Pool. The lower half dozen beats are short, ranging from 50 to 250 meters in length. Beats double and triple in length upstream from Beat 9, Murdo's Pool, and the stream gradient increases.

Dowsett handed Bob a landing net and a rod and assigned him Beat 8, Falls Pool. I was assigned Beats 4 and 5, Cemetery and Shinty. Dowsett then spent several minutes giving Bob directions to his beat, before finally exclaiming, "It's marked!" in response to Bob's blank look.

"Be careful not to hook the yellow and green electrified wire put up to keep cattle out of the river," Dowsett yelled after Bob, before saying to me, "He doesn't seem to have fish sense." I wondered if Dowsett was afraid of losing Bob to injury or heart attack after he also shared, "His complexion doesn't look good."

I walked over to Shinty Pool, crawled under a wire fence, and took position on a high grassy bank. Dowsett stood at my side, landing net strapped to his back. I made several practice casts to a slow-moving, peat-stained pool, cautious of low-lying obstacles within reach of a backcast. Once satisfied I knew how to handle a fly rod, Dowsett instructed me to let the fly swing across the tailout. A large dark Salmon, easily 10 pounds, showed several yards downstream, but a half hour of casting did not produce a take. After switching to a tube fly adorned with guinea hackle, I felt a gentle tug. A small Sea Trout on the end of my line shook its head and was off.

The next few hours passed quickly. I worked downstream along a badly eroded mud bank. Bright sunlight peeking through ominous gray clouds made me conscious of my shadow. However, wearing knee-high rubber boots prevented wading to the opposite shore. I switched to a weighted red hackle fly when another salmon broached the surface. What followed was two "pickups" or "grabs" on consecutive casts. *Was it a Salmon or another Brownie?* I wondered. Switching flies once again, I attracted a small Brownie that chased the offering to my feet. By now my internal clock had kicked in and I sensed time was running out. My half-day on the River Snizort came to an abrupt halt when Dowsett spotted Bob walking our direction. "Any luck?" we asked, as Bob approached.

"I saw several fish roll in the first pool, so I stayed there the entire time," he replied.

"I was afraid he would do that," Dowsett said under his breath.

We escorted Bob to the main gate where Dowsett pointed him to Beat 3. "Walk back to the highway bridge when you're finished," he said, "not where we parked the truck, because nobody will be there."

"I guess we were blanked," Dowsett said to me, on the hike up the hill to his truck. "You call it skunked, right?"

"Blanked sounds better," I replied.

Dowsett gifted me a pair of hand-tied Salmon flies, a pattern called the "Dowsett Dog" by the ghillie who designed it. It's an attractive pattern: No. 8 double hook, red guinea hen belly, copper wire thorax, and small bunch black rabbit wing sprinkled with gold tinsel. After losing one on a rock in the Hanford Reach of the Columbia River, I loaned the second to a buddy who tied up a couple of spares. I haven't caught a steelhead on the Dowsett Dog yet, but when I do, Derek Dowsett will be the first to know.

A few things need be shared with anglers having aspiration to visit the land of single malts, ghillies, and Sea Trout. First and foremost, you have no control over the weather and whether flows will be favorable or fresh run Salmon will be in the river when you arrive. Be sure to line yourself up with a qualified ghillie and obey the rules of private land ownership. Having previous experience angling for steelhead provides most of the skill you need to hook up with a Scottish Salmon.

I hope to return to the Isle of Skye and its River Snizort some day. When I do, I will bring my two-handed Spey rod, waders, an assortment of gear, several steelhead flies, and spend more days fishing. I'd like to book the Gate House, a furnished two-angler abode located a short stroll from the six lower beats. The Gate House rented for a modest 420 quid a week in 2017. It's a short stroll from the Skeabost Country House, where I can treat Nancy to a four-course dinner every night and still come out ahead on the deal.

The Dowsett Dog is a handsome fly.

More Recipes from the PANTRY

WHITEFISH CAVIAR

Remove the developing roe sacs or eggs from a large "hen" whitefish in pre-spawning condition and cut them into 2-inch or so sized chunks. Individual eggs will be small, on the order of 3 mm ($1/8$ inch) in diameter. Brine the eggs for 5 to 10 minutes in a mixture of ½ cup Kosher salt to 1 quart of ice-cold water. Once eggs have soaked up the proper amount of salt (Give them a taste test after 5 minutes so they don't get too salty), remove them from the brine and rinse with cold water. The attached membrane can be removed with your fingers or via a warm water rinse, after which you place the eggs in a glass bowl for another taste test. The skein of early developing roe is more difficult to process than mature roe that has begun to "loosen."

After the roe has achieved the proper amount of "saltiness," place loose eggs in a glass jar, seal, and store in the refrigerator. Homemade caviar can be stored in this manner for up to a week without significant loss of flavor. Don't expect the end product to look like blackish sturgeon caviar. Whitefish caviar is glossy, jewel-like orange, almost too pretty to eat. Serve with a selection of gourmet crackers and crème fraiche for a unique holiday treat.

SCOTTISH OATS WITH WHISKEY AND CREAM

Place a full cup of whole grain oats into a pan of 1-¾ cups boiling water, add a pinch of salt, stir, and lower the temperature to simmer for five minutes. Spoon the cooked oats into your favorite breakfast bowl, add a generous shot of single-malt whiskey, top with a dollop of cream, and follow with a tablespoon or two of brown sugar. This hearty bowl of cereal is guaranteed to maintain the rhythm in your Spey casting on a cold and windy day.

ACKNOWLEDGMENTS

I THANK GRANDPA HARRY for passing on his love for fly fishing and my two brothers, Dusty and Daran, who took me along. I am especially grateful to my wife, Nancy, for compiling the recipes and reviewing each story to ensure that I didn't get too full of myself. Several individuals contributed to these stories through their able companionship, inspiration, and/or factual review, including Derek Dowser, Dick Ecker, Mark Freshley, Ken Gano, Bill Hanf, Henry Hughes, Geoff McMichael, Ted Poston, Ron Reed, Grant Richey, Ben Romans, and Bill Rickard. Bev Johnston lent an editorial eye. Any errors in punctuation and grammar are mine.

Cover and layout design are by Laura Wahl. Illustrations are by the creative eye and capable hand of Ron Reed. The back page photo is by Ray Vermillion of Lucky Strike Fishing. The photo of the Dowsett Dog is by Ken Gano. All other photos, including the cover, are the author's.

Parts of some stories appeared in different form elsewhere: "Where Speckled Trout Live" in *American Angling*; "Spirit Mountain" and "Big Dog and Salmon Flies" in *Game & Fish*; "Beads and Bottlenose" and "Humpies Aren't Just for Grandchildren" in *Salmon-Trout-Steelheader*; "Back to Lugar Springs" and "Huckleberry Love" in *Northwest Fly Fishing*; "Car Body Beach" in the *Tri-City Herald*. Names of some individuals were altered within normal limits of discretion.

OTHER BOOKS BY DENNIS DAUBLE

Available at regional bookstores • Online at Amazon.com or KeokeeBooks.com

FISHES OF THE COLUMBIA BASIN
A guide to their natural history and identification

For any Northwest fisherman or woman on a quest for fishes and the places they live, *Fishes of the Columbia Basin* is an indispensable guide. Dennis Dauble, a fisheries biologist and lifelong fisherman himself, answers familiar questions and provides a comprehensive and detailed natural history of 60-plus species in the second edition of this popular field guide.

Nonfiction, 212 pages, 147 illustrations, glossary, list of fish species, index and 16 pages of color plates

THE BARBLESS HOOK
Inner sanctum of angling revealed

In this collection of stories drawn from a lifetime of fishing experiences, Dennis Dauble explores a range of topics anglers often don't discuss – trespassing, giving up a secret hole, losing fish at the net, competition between buddies and more While sometimes exposing what might be considered the "dark side of angling," Dauble manages to both entertain and inspire anglers in his first collection of fishing tales.

Nonfiction, 148 pages

ONE MORE LAST CAST
On the addictive nature of fishing

What do tiny bars of complimentary soap, spam sandwiches and pillow hogs have to do with fishing? When does one more "last cast" beget another? How can some people confuse fishing with ... sex? This collection of short stories answers those questions, and more, as author Dennis Dauble returns with more wry and humorous tales gleaned from a lifetime of fishing experiences and insights.

Nonfiction, 166 pages